Anna Clara Shute

Posthumous Poems

Anna Clara Shute

Posthumous Poems

Reprint of the original, first published in 1875.

1st Edition 2024 | ISBN: 978-3-38538-378-4

Verlag (Publisher): Outlook Verlag GmbH, Zeilweg 44, 60439 Frankfurt, Deutschland
Vertretungsberechtigt (Authorized to represent): E. Roepke, Zeilweg 44, 60439 Frankfurt, Deutschland
Druck (Print): Books on Demand GmbH, In de Tarpen 42, 22848 Norderstedt, Deutschland

POSTHUMOUS POEMS

POSTHUMOUS POEMS

BY

ANNA CLARA SHUTE

LONDON

CHAPMAN AND HALL, 193, PICCADILLY

1875

PRINTED BY TAYLOR AND CO.,
LITTLE QUEEN STREET, LINCOLN'S INN FIELDS.

CONTENTS.

———◆———

POEMS, WRITTEN FROM FOURTEEN TO
SEVENTEEN INCLUSIVE.

POEMS OF CHILDHOOD,
WRITTEN FROM NINE TO THIRTEEN INCLUSIVE.

Contents.

TRANSLATIONS FROM THE GERMAN.

POEMS.

They say the Loved one's voice appears
Like distant bells in lovers' ears;
That children's prattle low and light
Is to the mother music bright,
That nightingales upon the trees
Sit rapt in their own melodies;
But nothing half so fair can be
And nothing half so sweet to me,
As when from out the treasured store
You choose the book oft read before,
And from the beauties hidden here
You choose our favourites, mother dear.

B

No other voice has learnt the art
To cull the gems from every part ;
To bring the diamond into day,
And cast the worthless paste away ;
To lead us on from great to higher ;
To touch with pathos, rouse with fire,
And wrest the truth from every line,
As yours possesses, mother mine.

And when the words are poor and old,
When thoughts are nerveless, love is cold ;
Then with your voice's melody
You turn the dross to gold for me.
The fountain sparkles in the light,
The birds are glad, the flowers are bright,
And all the picture dead before
Bursts into glorious life once more ;

So lies the mountain cold and bare,
So runs the gloomy streamlet there ;

But when the Sun appears again,
At morning fair or after rain,
Then casting off her widowhood
Where long the mountain sad has stood,
She decks herself in glorious sheen
And stands in purple like a queen,
While the grey brook—her tears erewhile—
Now gives her but a brighter smile.

Dear mother, may I ask a boon,
A little one and granted soon,
Only that if you chance to meet
These foolish verses at your feet,
Will you but lend your voice's sound
To hide the failings you have found,
And make them by your love for me
What in themselves they cannot be.

SONG.

In heaven when I was young
The wild birds sung,
And the blue bells grew
Till the woods were faint
With their sweet delicious scent;
And the breeze came and went,
And, oh! I was content
In heaven when I was young.

On earth now I am old,
The days are cold;
And the flowers lie crush'd
In the fields about,
With the cruel rain and rout
And the wind's storm and shout;
And, oh! my light is out
On earth now I am old.

OLD LETTERS.

Old letters, it was only yesterday
I found them lying in the scented desk ;
Not cast aside with other waifs and strays,
But bound in silken fetters tenderly
And hidden in the deep recess apart.

One was a woman's hand I saw at once,
The other was a man's, though frail and fair ;
The writing was as though the work of one
Whose character was not of iron or stone,
But cast by Nature in a gentler mould,
As though his mother's loving tenderness
Were stronger in him than his father's pride

    *   *   *   *   *   *

HIS LETTER.

" I lay this morning on the grass
  Beside the river quietly fair,
I watched the swallows come and pass,
  I felt the sunshine everywhere.

" And lying in that warmth and light,
  Where no cold wind could come between,
I said, ' My will is moulded quite,
  To speak my soul to Gwendoline.

" But now within this silent room,
  Where one pale taper droops and dies,
My spirit sinks beneath the gloom
  And all my day-born courage flies.

" The words I draw from depths below,
  Uprooted from my heart with pain,
Too heavy with my sighs I know,
  Fall backward down the gulf again.

" As when by chance a fisher's spoils
    Are mixed with shells and seaweed grey,
The useless rubbish rends the toils
    And casts the good and bad away.

" Such weighty fears, Dear Heart, are mine
    That when my love would use its wings,
Those wings too gently formed and fine
    Are held on earth by grosser things.

" Alas ! alas ! I ramble on.
    My words are dust from prison bars,
And yet one smile of yours, sweet sun,
    Would turn the motes to shining stars.

" My heart was once a barren place,
    A hold of vice, a baneful den ;
But when I saw your angel face,
    The evil spirit left me then.

" I swept the house, I decked the wall,
　　I opened wide the windows dim ;
I let heaven's glorious sunshine fall
　　On what was once so stained and grim.

" And then I said the place is clean,
　　And sin and doubt are purged away,
And all is ready for the queen,
　　Who comes to claim her own to-day.

" Oh ! foolish thought and useless toil,
　　You raised your skirts and crossed the street ;
I might have known you would not soil
　　With floors like mine your spotless feet.

" And yet if you had guessed, I think,
　　How then I risked and lost my whole,
You would have bent across the brink
　　To drag from death a drowning soul.

" For since my rooms are swept and bare,
   And no one comes the house to fill,
Its ancient lord will enter there,
   With seven spirits baser still.

" Do you remember years ago,
   When you and I were girl and boy,
Those fairy tales which once you know
   Made up our little wealth of joy ?

" At sunset when the summer gales
   Were rich with sound of evening chimes,
Have you forgotten, dear, the tales
   We used to read a thousand times ?

" And there was one we loved the most—
   I think we loved it most of all—
A wondrous tale of fiend and ghost,
   Of fai y sprite and giant tall.

" Some hapless knight by adverse fate
 Had fall'n beneath a sorcerer's might,
Who chained him to his palace gate
 For evil beasts to rend at night.

" Nine awful hours the prisoner spent
 With weighted chains on every limb,
Each lingering hour that came and went
 Was like a hundred years to him.

" Nine awful hours, till night had grown
 And stars looked down with wolfish eyes,
And tree and bush and stock and stone
 Were changed to shuddering mysteries.

" And then when midnight clocks began,
 There came a sound of gathering feet,
And he, that cold undaunted man,
 Stood sternly forth his fate to meet.

" A glaring light, a widening din,
   A sobbing sound from snarling teeth,
He hears the hideous work begin,
   He feels the fetters snap beneath.

" A weight has fallen upon his breast,
   Soft breathings flit across his face—
His loved one's arms are round him prest,
   Her trembling hands his own embrace.

" And then — but, love, you know the rest,
   The knight was saved and all was joy ;
It was the tale we loved the best
   When you and I were girl and boy.

" O Gwendoline, the thing was true ;
   A shadowing forth of days to come—
I feel the doomed one's pangs anew ;
   Like him I stand unmoved and dumb.

" And heavy chains have numbed my might,
　　Whose links are former sins accurst,
And fiends must rend my soul by night,
　　Except you come to save me first.

" Oh ! by your love, which once was mine ;
　　By woman's pity, Christian faith,
By all things human and divine,
　　Stretch forth and snatch my soul from death."

HER LETTER.

" The golden light was falling wide,
　　Like gleams of Heaven's reflected flame,
And all was glorious evening-tide
　　When yesterday your letter came.

" The sky was all that spotless blue
　　Which smiled on Eden's bowers of old,
Save down the west where clouds renew
　　A world of red and pink and gold.

Old Letters.

" The birds were hushed, they did not sing,
   But here and there some wanderer's throat,
Who reached his nest on wearied wing,
   Would chirp a happy quivering note.

" Such stillness brooded near and far ;
   I watched and hardly dared to breathe.
Above, the Virgin Evening Star
   Seemed scarce more pure than earth beneath ;

" And whilst the tears I could not stay,
   Had veiled my eyes in glistening haze,
My being passed in prayer away
   And all my soul went forth in praise.

" And then it was when earth and heaven
   Were almost words which meant the same,
When God was Love and man forgiven,
   To break the spell your letter came.

" I read of Death, the child of Sin,
 And anguish born of black Despair,
Till Heaven again seemed hard to win,
 And sorrowing Earth no longer fair.

" Oh ! Bertram, once I loved you well,
 We loved as children years ago ;
How much I grieved, I cannot tell,
 To watch my playmate fall so low.

" But, since you write of childish days,
 Of former love and thoughtless youth,
For those old times' remembered ways,
 Be still, and hear me speak the truth.

" A withering blight, a deadly stain,
 Of late has fallen on England's sons,
A blinding veil, a maddening pain,
 Which light and hope and wisdom shuns.

" He comes by night, that demon fierce,
  Whén earth is dark and stars are not,
When moons no more the clouds can pierce,
  And man seems lost and God forgot.

" He whispers words of deadly aim,
  He scoffs at heavenly love and might,
Denies the source from whence you came,
  And names you child of chance and night.

" He takes you from a Father's care,
  He makes the world a casual heap ;
Hap-hazard, scattered here and there,
  The stars their aimless courses keep.

" The flower that blooms, the bird that sings,
  The spheres that dance around the sun,
Are so much clockwork, wheel and springs,
  Machinery ; but made by none.

" The restless sea, the patient lake,
    The hills which sleep through sun and shade,
All live by laws they cannot break ;
    Whence came the laws which no one made ?

" Your atheist boasts, your empty shows,
    Your new-born creed you think so grand,
Are like the wiles the ostrich knows,
    Who hides her head beneath the sand.

" She hears a voice, she turns and flees,
    She blinds her eyes in sand-heaps dun,
And thinks because she no one sees,
    That she herself is seen by none.

" Oh, cousin Bertram, learn belief,
    For faith alone can make us wise,
Our time on earth is all too brief,
    To pierce through heaven's mysteries.

" But she the gentle teacher, Faith,
 Who found us lisping children here,
Will guide us through the gates of death
 Till sight shall make the lesson clear.

" I would not blame, I only pray
 That He whose wisdom is not ours,
Will lead you in his own good way,
 From earthly weeds to heavenly flowers.

" And if you think my words unkind,
 Forgive me, for I needs must speak ;
But humbly to the master-mind,
 For you are strong as I am weak.

" Yet truth is strong, and speak I must,
 Lest truth on earth should cease to live ;
But if you think my words unjust,
 Again I ask you to forgive."

HIS LETTER.

" I will not speak of lover's zeal,
    Of heart-devotion strong and true;
But I will tell you what I feel,
    And how I came to think with you.

"You call me blind, you call me base,
    As one beneath a withering curse;
A man without a hope of grace,
    An Atheist or something worse.

" But, Gwendoline, you do me wrong,
    The man you paint—I once was he;
But creeds are weak, where love is strong,
    And Heaven was merciful to me.

" For when I learnt to know you first,
    My doctrine paled to worthless dross;
And all I long had fondly nursed
    Was turned to bitter dregs of loss.

" What were my books, my late delight,
  The forms to which my soul was wed!
The first faint star which shone at night
  Has taught me more than all I read.

" The whole creation spoke anew,
  A song of hope from every sod;
And so from them it passed to you,
  From you to Heaven, from Heaven to God.

" The love you bore your Lord was such,
  I held it shame to love Him less;
Till now I think I love as much,
  Such Godlike power has tenderness.

" Oh! best beloved, hear me plead,
  For this is truth if heaven is true;
And thus I learnt your faith indeed,
  And thus I came to think with you.

" I do not ask for love or hope,
   I only ask to be believed ;
The wretch whose neck must feel the rope,
   Yet finds his dying words received.

" In truth I am not half so base,
   As your harsh thought would make me be ;
I ask for justice, not for grace ;
   For audience, not for sympathy.

" Yet if at last you judge my crime,
   And find me hateful as before ;
Then give me but a little time,
   And you shall see my face no more."

HER ANSWER.

" I will render to your keeping,
Doubts at rest, and memory sleeping ;
Joy and grief, and smiles and weeping—
All a woman has to give.

I will never, dearest, never,
Heart or hope from you dissever;
Yours for ever and for ever!"'

FORGOTTEN.

How long I lay, how long I cannot say,
But at the last I woke, and though the dark
Wrapped all my limbs and held them stiff and
    stark,
  I knew that it was day.

  I felt the mountains tottering overhead,
I heard the hiss of waters, quenched in flame,
From east, west, north, and south, the nations
    came,
  And I alone was dead.

Great God! how long I waited! Still the call
Of trumpets rang sonorous,— still I said,
" It needs must take full time to wake the dead ;
   Not yet aroused are all."

At last was silence ; then there came a voice,
" Well done," He said, " good servants faithful
      shown,
Henceforth a place is yours around my throne,
   Rejoice, my friends, rejoice."

When that I heard, I could no longer wait,
An agony of fear my hopes did chase,
The Christ was portioning out to each his place,
   And I should be too late.

I strove to rise to force my coffin's lead,
To cry for help, to shriek in my despair,
I could not move a limb, nor breathe a prayer,
   For I was cold and dead.

And once again He spoke—" A curse of sin !
O ye, who shut your eyes, and would not see
What part or portion have you gained in me ?
   You may not enter in."

   With that there came a sobbing shriek of
      pain,
And cries and weeping, like a world in tears,
Till drowned in singing from a thousand spheres,
   It dropped nor rose again.

   O happy souls in Heaven's courts that dwell,
That live and move and ever see His face !
O happy they that *live* in any place,
   E'en though that place be Hell !

   The last archangel's trump had died away,
The tortured world was all ablaze with fire,
The melted ores were bubbling higher, higher,
   A stiffened corpse I lay.

O Death! on me alone your jaws you feed.
On me alone, O Death, you keep control ;
Closer than man to wife or flesh to soul,
   We two are bound indeed.

  Help, help, O Saviour, help! The world grows
      hot,
O lost, forsaken world. He is not there.
My punishment is more than I can bear ;
   Just God! Forgot, Forgot!

A GIRL'S RESOLVE.

I WILL not wed a common man,
  Whose heart is in his money,
Who rears the rose with thought and plan,
  But only recks the honey;
Who toils and slaves from dawn to dew,
  And calls it righteous labour,
Who grinds the mass and dowers the few,
  And thinks he loves his neighbour.

I will not wed a lady's pet,
  The dear delightful creature,
Too fond of horses, deep in debt,
  But perfect as to feature;

Or him I think they like as well,
   The most authentic parson,
With guides to Heaven and maps of Hell
   And antidotes for arson.

I will not wed a man whose heart
   Is withered ere his hair is,
His boast to own no shrine apart,
   No country and no lares ;
Who holds it wise from dawn to night
   To drain the goblet pleasure,
And takes at last the Shunamite
   To warm his torpid leisure.

But should I meet perchance with one
   Who doubts not God in mystery,
To whom the tale of great things done
   Is something more than history ;

Who, living in this travelled age,
  Still loves his hearth and nation,
And thinks and acts in silence sage
  To help his generation.

Whose heart is brave, whose will is strong,
  ·In earnest altogether;
He loves the right, he hates the wrong,
  He fears no stormy weather ;
His laugh is light, his voice is clear,
  He walks in strength and beauty,
And Truth is more than Honour dear,
  And more than Glory—Duty.

And should he, being more than this
  (Yea more, that slaves deride him),
Yet come and take my hand in his,
  And lead me forth beside him.

Oh ! then, through years and change and death,
  I'd walk and never waver,
My love should strengthen hope and faith,
  And make the bravest braver.

SONG.

When Lucy used to shun me,
I thought the winter's breath
Had withered June to death ;
I thought the flowers of May
Had shrunk from earth away,
That lovers' hopes and fears
Were nought but wasted years,
And bitter salt as tears,
 When Lucy used to shun me.

When Lucy said she loved me,
O then the skies above
Seemed hot and pale with love ;
O then the summer trees
For kisses wooed the breeze,
The birds went singing by,
They loved as well as I,
O happy earth and sky !
When Lucy said she loved me.

THE GRANDMOTHER'S STORY.

Come close to the fire, dear Amy,
  With your stool beside me so,
And I'll tell you a tale, my darling,
  Of my childhood long ago.

The logs on the hearth are blazing,
  Till the pictures glitter and shine,
And your little face in the twilight
  Looks pleadingly up into mine.

The wind with the clouds is battling,
  Till the pine-trees shake with fear ;
Is it the storm or the darkness,
  Which has made the past so clear ?

I see a room in the fire-light,
  And a sailor bearded and browned,
And a woman in tears beside him,
  And the children clinging around.

I see the moment of parting,
  With its struggle and passionate sighs,
With its kisses and broken blessings,
  And sobbings and choking replies.

But the ship is weighing her anchor,
  The Captain must do his part,
And the wife must be left to her anguish,
  With her children clasped close to her heart.

D

He sailed, but he wrote so often,
  Such wonderful things he had seen,
Blue birds of Paradise flashing,
  And the dolphins leaping between.

And fairy green isles on the ocean,
  And flowers afloat from the shore ;
Oh, how we lived in his letters !
  Till at last they came no more.

We heard of gales to the southward,
  And of wrecks and sinking ships ;
And my mother's cheeks grew whiter,
  And the smile died away from her lips.

She pined and drooped like a flower,
  As the terrible weeks went round,
But she neither wept nor fainted,
  When they told her he was drowned.

She took us all to her bosom,
  The sobbing fatherless things,
As a dove, when her mate is stricken,
  Still shelters her young with her wings.

She led us out from our cottage,
  To seek a home in the west,
She fasted for bread to feed us,
  She toiled that we might have rest.

And years went on, and the children
  Grew merry of heart and light ;
All day the mother was cheerful,
  But she cried through half the night.

One evening late in the autumn,
  We sat by the fire-light so,
My sisters and I were spinning,
  And Willie was whistling low.

My mother sat in the shadow,
  And her hand was over her eyes,
And our whispers had sunk to silence,
  As the flame there sinks and dies.

Little Lucy had crept beside me,
  Her golden head on my knees,—
Hush! was it a voice in the darkness,
  Or only the wind in the trees?

My mother had stirred for a moment,
  Then sank in the shadow once more;
And, hark! through the rush of the tempest
  There came a knock at the door.

"Some traveller who seeks a shelter,"
  My mother said, "from the storm;
Go, Frank, and bid him enter,
  And heap the logs up warm."

A hasty voice at the threshold,
　A hasty foot on the stair,
And a form at the open doorway,
　And a cry, and a sob, and a prayer.

My mother knelt in the fire-light,
　Her arms round the stranger's neck,
'Twas my Father, my own dear Father,
　Whom God had saved from the wreck.

This is the tale of my childhood,
　I read when the fire gets low,—
Don't cry, it was years ago, dear,
　Years upon years ago.

BOLD RESOLUTIONS.

WHAT shall I do to grace the day
When my true love comes by this way ?

I'll twist a ribbon in my hair,
The shade he loves me best to wear.

I'll dash my eyes with tears for dew
Till stars shine out amidst their blue.

I'll bathe my cheeks in blushes warm
As bright as sunshine after storm.

I'll walk in white from head to toe,
Because he said I pleased him so.

I'll fill the rooms with garlands gay,
Primroses, and buds of May.

I'll bide at home and watch and wait,
To see him coming through the gate.

I'll set the door and windows wide,
To hear his ringing voice outside.

I'll run to meet and hail him King
And lead him in and laugh and sing.

He comes at last at close of day,—
O hide me, hide me safe away.

NIGHT.

How sweet it is to rest at night,
With all one's sins forgiven quite;
With folded hands and pillowed head,
The peace of death without its dread!

When all unwatch'd and low I lie,
To think of angels guarding by,
Till in the hush that darkness brings,
I almost hear their brushing wings.

To watch the hours that leapt by day,
Come stealing like a cat this way;
So velvet soft their step and slow,
I scarce can hear them gliding go.

Or all alone with no one near,
To feel a sudden gasp of fear,
And sob, my head all sheeted white,
" O Father, shield Thy child to-night."

Then strange and sweet the while I pray,
The dark seems brimming o'er with day,
And One, I think, draws near my bed,
Who had not where to lay His head.

And like a thief when help is nigh
The evil spirits turn and fly ;
My sheltered room is hallowed land,
With Strength and Safety close at hand.

So silent Earth, and Heaven so near,
If Death came now I could not fear ;
But thought of death has made me weep,
And so in tears I fall asleep.

THE PORTENT.

WHAT can help a once great soul,
When she falls from Heaven to hell?
Angels once that loved her well,
Weeping, leave her where she fell.
   Weeping cannot make her whole,
Cannot raise her whence she fell,
   Are her wings for ever broken?
Must the darkness ever bind
All the travail of the mind,
   All the truths she might have spoken?
Not for ever—Heaven is kind—
   Doubters, listen to the token.

Waking at night from feverish dreams,
I saw how the moon in long white gleams,
   On the mountain's face
     Lay weird and tall,
   Till, like the trace
     Of the hand on the wall,
Each cottage stood out with a front as white
As the ghosts that peer through the dark at night.

   Though the east was dense,
     In its own wild way,
   The light was intense
     As the maniac's day.
The moon she was hidden behind the house,
But her lover, the wind, in mad carouse
  Was chasing her round the roofs ;
I could see her hand on the mountain's base,
I could hear his shouts as he followed apace,
  And the tramp of his heavy hoofs ;
But the white of her face I could not see,
And the cold of his touch it reached not me.

The length of the house, like the shadow of death
Stretched waste and deep to the edge of the glare ;
And earth was heavy with graves beneath,
And nameless things had poisoned the air,
I hid my head for I dared not sleep.
    And the moon dropped red,
      In the jaws of the west,
    And the storm lay dead,
      On the earth's cold breast,
And darkness fell on the face of the deep.
A little moment of endless dread,
And then of a sudden I turned my head,
And I saw through the window where I lay,
How night had passed with its fever away,
And gentle and quiet and grey
Rose the new day.

A LOVER'S QUARREL.

THE roses are blooming without in the sun,
Come forth, O my love, in the warm summer
    grass,
The wild doves are cooing, the butterflies wooing,
And a thousand young blossoms smell sweet as
    we pass,
And Willy shall come now his lessons are done,
And sweet little Katy her father's own lass.

I have set you your seat at the edge of the firs,
And your sketchbook and brushes beside you are
    laid,
And great crimson berries of ruddy ripe cherries,

And plums with the down on, are stored in the
　　shade,
And Katy shall sing us that new song of hers,
And Willy shall read us the tale he has made.

＊　　＊　　＊　　＊　　＊　　＊

Oh ! do you remember, or have you forgot,
The day of our quarrel which cost us such tears ?
Young Harry the sailor, escaped from his jailer,
Had been telling the tale of his flight and his
　　fears,
The Russian's pursuit and the fast-falling shot,
And the bitter-cold night on the desolate meres.

He lay on the grass in the shade of the trees,
You bent down above him, you flushed through
　　your veil,
Your eyes as they listened, they flashed and they
　　glistened,
Your lips all a-tremble now red and now pale ;

The tears to your eye-lids had crept by degrees,
You trembled, you triumphed, you lived in his
    tale.

I had left you in anger, I watched from the door ;
The blood in my temples throbbed wicked and
    wild,
His words were a blessing, his looks a caressing ;
I knew that he loved you, I felt that you smiled,
And, oh ! how I cursed him a thousand times o'er,
When you leant on his shoulder and laughed like
    a child.

That night in the ball-room your step was so
    light,
Your eyes were so happy, your voice was so clear,
Your colour grew brighter, your footsteps were
    lighter,
I was sure,—I had marked it,—when Harry drew
    near ;

I crept to the window away from men's sight,
And I watched you in anger, and envy, and fear.

At last you drew near me, you passed where I
    stood,
You saw me and stopped, with a pretty surprise.
" Oh, Frank I have found you !   The curtains
    were round you,
You were hid like a sulky old bear from our eyes.
A valse is beginning, come dance and be good,
On music like this I could float to the skies."

You leant on my arm with a little caress,
Your sweet sunny eyes all a-dancing with glee ;
I only grew colder to feel on my shoulder,
The soft little hand that I loved so to see.
You looked like a child in your white muslin dress,
But you seemed like a false-lipped enchantress
    to me.

And, then, you remember that Harry came by,
Attuned to the music and flushed with the ball,
And two minutes after in frolic and laughter
You were whirling together the maddest of all ;
I turned on my heel with a half-uttered cry,
And the thoughts of my breast were as bitter as
 gall.

Next morning I sat in my study and read,
Read Plato and Kant, and the words of the wise,
Yet still all the printing was glowing and glinting,
With the light of two innocent hazel-brown
 eyes.
I turned at the sound of your soft little tread,
And I watched you draw near, with a sullen
 surprise.

You came in so softly and stood by my chair,
Like a child who is naughty and longs to be
 good ;

E

The pretty, arch teasing, half-wicked, half-
pleasing
Was quenched in your eyes by your sweet sorry
mood,
And the one crimson rose you wore in your
hair,
It scarcely blushed deeper than you as you
stood.

" Dear Frank, are you angry ? What is it I've
done ?
I see that you shun me, I cannot tell why ;
Is it Captain O'Lary, or Ernest, or Harry ?
Are you vexed that I danced with that stupid Sir
Guy ?
Be my priest, let me go through my sins every
one,
But stoop to absolve me, dear Saint, by-and-
by."

I sprang to my feet and I thrust you aside,
'' Enough of this acting for you and for me !
Reserve all these graces and sweet double faces,
These blushes and blamings for Harry to see ! "
" You are mad ! you insult me ! Be silent ! " you
    cried ;
" Take back your false promise, henceforth you
    are free ! "

You sprang to the door like a bird from the
    hand,
But you showed me your face as you flitted
    away ;
The fire that was in it quite hushed for a minute
The host of wise things I was ready to say ;
For anger and pride and disdainful command,
Had turned your young face to a terror that day.

I left the old house by the slow flowing Trent,
And I sped to the North with a friend and a gun,

All day through the heather we plodded together,.
We chased the red stag till the set of the sun ;
And back to the cottage at even we went,
As tired as the peasant whose labour is done.

At last when I thought I had learned to forget,
There came from the southward a letter from
      Mills ;
A gossiping letter—" He sent me a setter,
He wanted a pony to ride on the hills :
Mrs. Forbes had appeared in the Countess's set,
And Le Clerq had dishonoured Sir Newdigate's
      bills."

" You have heard, " so he wrote, " of the news of
      the day,
The hero from Russia has conquered anew ;
Young Harry O'Brien, that runaway lion,
Has boarded two eyes of the loveliest blue ;
And sweet Annie Murray has helped him they say,
And so I've no doubt she has told it to you."

Then fell there for ever the scales from my
    eyes,
And doubt and suspicion together had flown;
My dread and my danger was wooing a stranger,
The world was an Eden and Annie my own;
And Harry might win all the blue in the skies,
If he left but my sunshine of hazel alone.

How often I see in the dreams of the night
That plot of green lawn where the shadows were
    long;
Where manhood unheeded, I knelt and I pleaded,
Repented my folly, confessed I was wrong;
Till we fell to each other with a sob of delight,
With the passion of lovers so tender and strong.

My own! you are crying. My darling! my
    life!
Has the thought of our quarrel such sorrow to-
    day!

Have hailstorms of kisses as fervent as this is,
Yet never had power to wipe it away?
Has love no redemption?—Ah, Annie, my wife!
Your lips may say " No," but your life has said,
   " Yes."

A LAMENTATION.

This world is made to break our hearts !
We think at first the pleasant days
Will lead us on through even ways ;
And hope and pain, so balanced war,
That pain shall never claim to be
The lord by right of mastery
Of things that were and things that are ;
Then cometh sorrow with his darts,
And tears that blight, and doubt that parts,
And lurking love-nooks full of smarts :
This world is made to break our hearts !

What had he done that he must die?
Not his to pay the penalty;
For sin his life had never known,
His youth's white flower was all his own.
What had he done that he should die?
He did not die as He of old,
Who gave His life to save His fold,
Who died for us on Calvary.
He died to make his mother moan,
And loathe her life and curse the years;
He died to draw his sisters' tears
And make their sunny eyes grow dim,
And leave the hearts that loved him lone.
He died,—for God had need of him,
And Christ was yearning for His own.

A THANKSGIVING.

How good the world is, beautiful,
   With God's own finger fair,
With smooth green hills, and forests cool,
   And birds that beat the air;
With sweet spring-flowers that stir and wake,
   Because the breeze goes by,
And little leaves that dance and shake
   Against the summer sky.

And I to-day as happy am
   As maid a fortnight wed,
As student by the banks of Cam
   With late belaurelled head;

As mother with her first-born child,
   To worship and to bless,
As lover thinking how she smiled,
   When first she whispered " Yes."

The gates of melody are burst,
   I sing for very weal;
The notes ring out as when at first,
   A child, I heard them peal;
And down beneath the pines I fell,
   My knees against the sod,
With Nature's choir I sang as well,
   My song of praise to God.

But since that time a rugged gain
   Had held my lips in awe,
For knowledge teaching all my stain
   Had taught me to withdraw;

No more the friend of bud and flower,
  And unabashed as they,
Like Adam, in the twilight hour,
  I hid my face to pray.

To-day at last my doubts are still,
  I walk and know no fear,
The tokens of a Father's will,
  Are round me far and near ;
And happy through the fields I pass,
  Where pleasant waters flow,
His hands have touched the meadow grass,
  And bade the lilies blow.

When first my sun of gladness broke,
  I could not speak or smile,
But like the sleeper first awoke,
  I lay and hushed awhile ;

And softly to myself I said,
  " The tide of grief is slow,
But soon it dashes o'er its bed,
  And joy may too be so."

And so it was, as still in sleep,
  Two dream-like days went by,
And all at once with bound and leap,
  The golden flood ran high ;
It swept my feet, it reached my knee,
  It dashed my hands apart,
Till on the billows wild and free
  I floated bold of heart.

They bear me up those waters bright,
  They wash my fears away,
The rainbow of a Father's might,
  Is in the clouds to-day.

My happiness! my happiness!
　O God! to Thee I call,
To earth and heaven Thy name I bless,
　And bless Thy hand in all.

Full oft-times in my common lot,
　I strove my harp to tune,
But awe too deep, or shame too hot,
　Has dimmed the music soon.
Full oft-times in the hush of grief,
　I bowed yet dared not pray,
Behold! with bird and bud and leaf,
　I sing! I sing to-day!

WHAT THE FLUTE BROUGHT.

THE Artist played on his well loved-flute,
Till all around were hushed and mute;

For he breathed forth notes so full and clear,
That men and women wept to hear;

And he sang of life and of human lot,
Till time and being were all forgot;

And each one thought within his breast
Of the thing on earth he loved the best.

The Painter thought of his growing fame,
And the work that should give him an endless
name.

The Poet was trembling with heaven-born might,
And he prayed for strength to use it right.

The Scholar was dreaming of heights to climb,
And knowledge snatched from the gulfs of Time.

The Priest, like a saint, sat calm and grey,
And prayed for the soul he had saved that day.

The Maiden was thinking of books and friends,
And of fair green paths with unknown ends.

The Lover he walked in Paradise,
By a sweet young face with its clear blue eyes.

The Father groaned for he saw once more,
The little grave by the churchyard door ;

But the Mother pressed his hand and smiled,
As she thought of Heaven and her angel child.

THOUGHTS ABOUT THOUGHTS.

As on my bed I wakeful lie,
And watch the night-hours crawling by,
And cannot sleep, I know not why !

A thousand thoughts of joy or pain
Come pressing by, an endless train ;
They pass and never come again.

Some, beautiful as angel's wing,
Tuneful as notes the blackbird sings,
Bright as the tints the autumn brings.

And some are deep, too deep to scan,
And some are tremulous and wan,
With distant hopes too wide for man.

And others, which I dare not name,
With whispered words of pride and blame,
Disguised as thought the Tempter came.

But grand or base, across my soul,
The tide of thought without control,
Wave after wave I watched it roll.

And while I mark them gliding past,
I wonder whence they haste so fast,
And what the goal they reach at last.

The thanewho saw the sparrow loom,
One moment through the lighted room,
Then flutter forth again to gloom ;

F

He well compared the bird to man.
We cannot look beyond his span,
Nor know we whence his course began.

And so to me it often seems,
These night-born thoughts which are not
    dreams,
Flash like the bird where fire-light gleams.

We mark them glittering in the light,
One moment shine they broad and bright,
Then hasten out again to night.

But now to-day I seem to hear
A voice that whispers very near,
Its words have made the mystery clear.

" Each separate thought your mind creates,
That passes on and never waits,
Is big with meanings, deep with fates.

" From man's infinitude of soul,
Each thought arises, and its goal
A place where angels hold control.

" There good and bad alike have sway,
The good can only teach and pray,
They cannot thrust the bad away.

" Your guardian angel ready stands,
And gives you forth with willing hands,
The very flower your work demands.

" Each opened flower of thought you know,
Within your soul you watched it blow,
But deemed it perished long ago.

" These blossoms spring from former seeds ;
The angel black of evil deeds,
Whence did he call those briars and weeds ?

" Each for himself his crown must frame,
The flowers or weeds will loud proclaim
Alike his glory or his shame."

DOLLY'S POEM.

What is little Dolly doing,
  Stealing from the rest away ?
Bow and arrow, cricket, croquet,
  All have lost their charm to-day.

With a monstrous sheet of foolscap,
  And a quill so fair and clean,
Dolly means to write a poem
  For her favourite magazine.

She will write for dear 'Aunt Judy,'
　　Such a beauty, all her own,
Not a word to Grace or Nelly,
　　She must make it quite alone.

She will make a wondrous fortune,
　　Like the great Sir Walter Scott;
Some to keep and some for presents,
　　Some for dear 'Aunt Judy's' cot.

Now she sits a little sadly,
　　For she cannot quite find out,
Though at first it seemed so easy,
　　What there is to write about.

See! she clasps her hands in triumph,
　　Pen and paper radiant takes,
She has found a glorious subject,
　　Good King Alfred and the cakes!

Counting backwards, counting forwards,
  Scratching out a hundred times,
Dolly thinks it very curious
  Where the poets find their rhymes.

On her little chubby fingers
  Every syllable she weighs,
Still the verse for all her trouble,
  Halts or gallops, lags or stays.

How to make a scold poetic,
  Little Dolly cannot think,
And from finding rhymes for " Goat-herd,"
  Tennyson himself might shrink.

Dolly, foolish little maiden !
  Leave your trying, off to play !
With your hopeless undertaking,
  You have wasted half the day.

Dolly's Poem.

Never mind the scribbled paper,
  Come and stand beside me so,
I will tell you in a whisper,
  Something Dolly does not know.

Though they cannot "make up verses,"
  Though they may not write a line,
Little children too are poems,
  Fresh and fragrant, Dolly mine.

When your kisses pout for answers,
  When your happy laughter chimes,
This is better far than verses,
  Sweeter than a poet's rhymes.

See the lilies toil and spin not,
  God has given to each his part ;
Little children too are poems,
  Writ in every good man's heart.

SUGGESTED BY A SERMON,

SEPT. 22ND, —72.

" There remaineth therefore a rest for the people of God."
HEBREWS.

To ye, my Christian brothers,
   The weary and distressed,
I come this Sabbath morning
   To speak to you of rest.
To ye who toil and languish,
   And faint all day for bread ;
Who long all day for even,
   And loathe the morning red ;
To ye I bring a message,
   Of summer days in store,
Whence pain and grief are banished,
   And tears shall be no more.

O, ye who walk as Christians,
   Whose heart the Lord hath blest ;
Ye know the joy I speak of,
   The boon of Sabbath rest.
To wake some sunny morning,
   When all the sky is blue,
And through the panes the roses
   Are shining in the dew.
To lie and hear the thrushes,
   And dream of Holy things ;
Till clouds against the ether
   Have turned to Angels' wings.
To know the six days' labour
   May leave our minds to-day,
And all our thought—devotion,
   And all our need—to pray.
This happy Sunday sunshine,
   This day of earth's the best.
Oh ! this is but the shadow
   Of Israel's Sabbath rest.

I know that work is noble,
 A good for high and low,
A thing to love and cherish,
 For God has willed it so ;
And none too little needed,
 Too poor for nature's plan ;
I think that God made daisies
 As earnestly as man.

But he whose work is truest,
 And he who toils the best ;
Best knows the joy I speak of,
 And sighs for Sabbath rest—
A rest from toil and longings,
 From want and gnawing care,
From doubtings and from dangers,
 From darkness and despair ;
A rest from outward struggles,
 And cruel strife within,

And, oh ! far more than either,
　Dear friends, a rest from sin.

To drop our rags and burden,
　Like Christians at the cross;
To meet the Saints in glory,
　Who held this world as loss ;
To kiss the Feet we worship,
　That once trod mortal sod ;
To lose and merge our being
　In God—my soul ! in God !

I see Him through the darkness,
　He calls us even now ;
A grave and mournful presence,
　With thorns about His brow ;
His arms are stretched to meet us,
　His voice has filled the place,
His words are full of comfort,
　And full of love His face.

" Oh! come to me, ye weary,
    Sore-laden and oppressed,
My yoke is light and easy,
    And I will give you rest."
And some pass on in silence,
    And some with mock and jeer ;
A few have stopped to listen,
    The meek of heart draw near.
His cross is on their foreheads,
    He takes them to His breast
And earth is all forgotten,
    And Christ, He gives them rest.
Oh ! Christ, our ears are opened,
    Our lips no longer dumb,
We feel Thee through the darkness,
    We come, dear Lord, we come.

HELEN'S CRAG.

THE moon on Helen's crag shone clear;
  The lonely crag where Helen died,
And up and down alone I walked,
  Beside the crawling tide.

The shadows stretched across the land,
  The light was strong on sky and sea,
The white sand shone, the moon looked on,
  As cold as cold could be.

'Twas such a night on such an hour
  When down the crag young Helen fell ;
A purple blot has marked the spot,
  The fishers mind it well.

And walking there, where once she walked,
  Her piteous tale to rhymes I strung ;
And this is what I found to say,
  While yet the night was young.

Sweet Helen ! Pride of all the vale,
  The fairest thing that eyes could see ;
And young Macdonald loved her well,
  No knight more brave than he.

And when he left her for the wars,
  He gave her first a blood-red flower,
A mountain rose that only grows
  On crags by Helen's bower.

"And take and keep this rose," he said,
　"'Twas got with toil and willing strain,
For down the steep with crawl and leap,
　I went this flower to gain.

"So keep it safe, and keep it true,
　A token sure as sure can be ;
For by this flower, whate'er accrue,
　I judge your love for me."

And months went on, and still afar,
　Macdonald waved the Highland flag,
And blood-red roses bloomed and died,
　In chinks on Helen's crag.

But still against a maiden's heart,
　Lay soft and warm a withered flower ;
And lips would press in mute caress
　Its leaves from hour to hour.

And so at last when nights were long,
    And winter's finger stroked the glass,
A Highland lad who rode like mad,
    Came dashing down the pass.

And off at Helen's feet he leapt,
    And down on bended knees he fell—
" The words I bear, my lady fair,
    God grant they please you well.

" Macdonald greets his lady sweet,
    And prays her by the love she owes,
Since evil fame would blast her name
    To send him straight the rose."

Then Helen sought her inmost bower,
    And lined with linen white and pure
A jewelled case in which to place,
    Her treasure safe and sure.

G

Then slowly from her bosom white
 She drew her flower with loving pride,
And in her joy to call the boy,
 She flung the window wide.

Ah, woe the day! For ships go down,
 Though friendly land be well in sight,
The north wind blew, the petals flew,
 Bescattered left and right.

Some lightly float, some reach the moat,
 Some borne by winds are tossed on high;
In Helen's hand the withered stalk
 Is glaring, stript, and dry.

Ah! well may Helen wring her hands;
 Her tears, her groans are all in vain,
The priceless flower, her joy, her dower,
 She'll never hold again.

While others slept, she watched and wept;
   A desperate hope had filled her breast,
And through the castle gates she crept,
   And down the steep she prest.

She heard the sullen waves that struck
   The sightless caverns' depths below,
The cold damp night had graspt her tight,
   And would not let her go.

And still she went, and still intent,
   She searched each bank and hidden cleft,
Perchance to find, the rocks behind,
   Some rose the storms had left.

The ocean groaned, the night wind moaned,
   The silent moon kept counsel well,
The path was steep, the chasm deep,
   Where Helen slipped and fell.

O, what avail though still in death,
A maiden clasps a withered rose !
For curst, I trow, the treacherous brow
Whereon that blossom grows.

They found her stretched along the beach,
A thing that death had still left fair ;
The waves were playing round her feet,
The seaweeds in her hair.

THE ENCHANTED SLEEP.

WHEN first the earth by God prepared,
   In new-born beauty stood,
With fish and beasts in order paired,
   And fowl—a numerous brood ;
" My work is done," the Lord declared,
   And saw that it was good.

But ere His crowning glory, Man,
   He set to rule the rest,
Ere noonday sun its course had run,
   Or evening stained the west,
He, whispering to His works, began
   To tell them His behest.

The twilight knew its time to rise,
　　The moon her lamp to light,
The stars that slept in daylit skies,
　　Would wake and shine at night ;
God's works had learnt their destinies,
　　And all had learnt them right.

But now to each He gave in dower
　　A secret gift and new :
The joyous earth with sudden power,
　　Was throbbing through and through ;
The smallest stone, the lowliest flower,
　　Were bright with promise too.

" Be glad," He said ; " the gift is good,
　　But not to be revealed ;
Rejoice but wait, ye restless flood ;
　　Be silent, laughing field ;
Through years of struggle, change, and blood,
　　Your secret keep concealed,

To each a separate time for rest,
　For waiting, I decree ;
Who guards his gift and hides it best
　Shows best his love for me.
Then open wide your fruitful breast,
　And tell your secret free."

He spoke, and all created things
　With deeds for words replied,
With folded leaves and brooding wings,
　The better all to hide ;
They sleeping kept through circling springs
　Their secret sanctified.

And years went on, though man grew wise,
　Through many a winter's day,
He only saw with outward eyes,
　Nor marked what buried lay,
Till truths, like buds of April skies,
　Burst forth and bloomed in May.

At first the horse, too free for fear,
   Went bounding bold alone,
Through golden grain untouch'd in ear,
   And wilds of grass unmown;
Till man with bit and scythe drew near
   And claimed them for his own.

At first the sheep retained her fleece,
   The flax her shining thread,
The wise-eyed cattle grazed in peace,
   The birds were safe o'erhead;
But winds are cold and wants increase,
   And children must be fed.

For long the giant in water slept,
   With fire charmed out by none,
Till called by genius forth it leapt,
   For Watt and Stephenson;
And strode the earth, and sprung the cleft,
   And joined the worlds in one.

For many a year their deadly bane,
  The lurking poisons gave ;
The lightning struck with burning stain—
  Till man arose to save;
And one he taught to soothe our pain,
  And one he bound his slave.

So one by one as years went by,
  The earth her secrets told ;
The ocean calls, the depths reply,
  The flowers their leaves unfold,
New stars are rising in the sky,
  Which never dawned of old.

The destined man so proud, so bold,
  His brave heart bounding free,
His prize more dear to him than gold,
  To all the world shows he—
" This beautiful young thing behold !
  Awoke to life by me."

LOVE'S SUMMER.

I was a withered, blasted tree
Till Love's sweet summer smiled on me;

It made me brave, it made me strong,
It filled my boughs with birds and song;

It made me bud and blossom wide,
So changed was I, the forest's pride.

The wrens and linnets loved me best,
I gave them twigs to build their nest;

I gave them moss to line them warm,
My leaves their roof in sun and storm.

From branch to branch the squirrels sprung,
They hid their pelf my boles among.

The patient cattle sought my shade,
Around my trunk the children played.

The startled echoes throbbed around,
With shouts of ' Whoop ' and ' Titler's Ground '.

And when the west was all aflame,
At silent eve the lovers came;

My mossy roots they made their seat,
The grass was soft beneath their feet.

Against my trunk she leant her head,
I felt the happy tears she shed ;

I hid them close from mortal eyes,
For love's sweet touch had made me wise.

I saw their lips for kisses thrill,
I heard their vows, and guard them still.

But when their words too eager grew,
I stretched my arms against the blue,

And cleaving wide my leafy crown,
I showed them Heaven gazing down.

A PRAYER.

O FATHER, help me, Father; stretch Thy hand
Give guidance to me blind, unloose me dumb,
That I may speak if thus Thy word decrees—
I know not, all the world is great with life,
That sobs and stumbles inarticulate words,
And yearns for voice, as one who cast on shore
By force of restless waves, gropes round and
    points,
And lacks for bread, without interpreter.
And is it I shall speak? Are words of mine
To gather close the threads of shapeless thought,

To weave, to shape, to give them back to men,
In new bright colours drest—combined—revealed ?
What strength is mine for this ? Am I the sun,
To gather vapours from the steaming earth ;
To bind them, paint them purple, gold, and red,
And send them down at last as fruitful rain ?
O Talent, rotting in the musty ground,
How useless, stained, and clogged with rust art
　　thou,
Most cumbrous, worthless, in a napkin laid !
Awake, O slumbering strength, if strength is there,
Lest some Delilah shear thine unkempt locks,
And steal thy might through idleness. Beware !
Thy strength may come too late, if once delayed,
And that which erst had set a people free,
And lashed their foes, and crushed their outlawed
　　gods,
Will serve thee but to ply a slave's full work,
To turn thy foeman's millstones, stand for sport
On Dagon's day in sinful heathen courts,

Or, mad for vengeance, drag their temple down,
And fell at once thy Conquerors and thyself,
O God! Thy will be mine, Thine arm my trust,
Teach Thou the words to speak, if speak I must.

THE LITTLE MERMAID.

LITTLE gentle, happy waves,
  Dancing, rippling, turning, swelling,
Say what race of kings or slaves
  Far beneath your light is dwelling,
Palaces, or fairy caves,
What conceal ye, gentle waves?

Is it true what I have read,
  How King Neptune reigns in splendour,
Fishes leap above his head,
  Tritons tall their homage tender,
Sportive nymphs around him dart,
Stirring light the monarch's heart?

Little wavelets fresh and bright,
  Have you seen those ocean portals,
Halls of coral red and white,
  Wondrous sights denied to mortals?
I have heard of mermaids, too,
Tell me, darlings, is it true?

Does she walk on silver sands
  Far below, the Sea King's daughter?
While her sisters join their hands,
  Laugh and shout and splash the water;
Only she no more is gay,
Cannot dance or sing to-day.

Changed the little mermaid's face,
  And her blue eyes dim with crying;
Changed since first in sportive race,
  Round the great ship anchored lying;
Floating near on waters dun,
She has seen the Land-King's son?

H

Music streaming from the deck,
 Dancers flying fast and faster,
Straining high her queen-white neck,
 She can see him whirling past her ;
And his voice in laugh and cheer,
Falls like joy bells on her ear.

Then the night, the storm, the rain,
 Sudden darkness, wind, and thunder,
Sail and rigging dashed in twain,
 Rope and cable rent asunder ;
Scarcely time to gasp and shrink,
Ere the ship must strike and sink.

Where the Prince lies pale and drowned,
 Floats unharmed the Sea King's daughter,
With her arms she clasps him round,
 Bears him gently through the water ;
On her breast his golden head—
" Sleep my beautiful," she said.

" Sleep and dream of arms of snow,
   Dream of couch as soft as this is."
Hour by hour she held him so,
   Warmed his poor pale lips with kisses ;
And the moon rose fair and grave,
As they floated on the wave.

All night long she held him fast,
   While the great waves drove them forward,
But when morning broke at last,
   Slow and sad she turned her shoreward ;
One soft kiss for brow and hand,
Ere she laid him on the sand.

Sad the little mermaid sits,
   Clasps her temples hot and throbbing,
Wrings her pretty hands by fits,
   Hides her head in tears and sobbing,
But when night has dimmed the blue,
Swift she soars the waters through.

Past the waste of shining sands,
   'Twixt the rocks and up the river,
Where the Palace mirrored stands,
   Where the lamps reflected shiver,
Where the Prince the stream beside,
Walks and whispers with his bride.

Little reck that princely twain,
   Deep in bliss of youth and maiden,
How she wrings her hands in pain,
   Strikes her bosom passion laden ;
Perhaps a boat or perhaps a swan,
Seemed to float the waves upon.

Quite forgot and out of mind,
   All that night of swift disaster,
When through stress of storm and wind,
   True and brave she held him faster ;
When her kisses cooled his brow,
Kiss and tears forgotten now.

Only sometimes when the tide
   Strikes the shore in measured season,
Turns he musing to his bride,
   " Sweet," he says " I know no reason,
But the ripples' whispers seem
Like the voices in a dream."

WRITTEN IN A FRIEND'S ALBUM.

AN angel was holding a half-open book,
    And the children in Heaven, like children on
        earth,
    Just as curious, came peeping, and cried out in
        mirth,
" Let us look, O good Friend, let us look ! "

For long he resisted, till one little maid,
    Climbed up on his shoulder, and there from her
        throne,
    Where laughing and fondling she nestled alone,
Turned over the leaves half afraid.

But soon she cried out with a burst of delight,
    " O Friend ! put me down, but give me the
      book,
    That my brothers and sisters may all come and
      look,
At this beautiful, beautiful sight."

So the Angel he lifted her down on the meads,
    And the children came running and pressing
      and peeping,
    For that book, is the loveliest angels are keeping,
And they call it The Book of Good Deeds.

There some were seen freeing the captives from
      fetters,
    Or feeding the hungry, or clothing the cold ;
    And others, whose faces were good to behold,
Were frankly forgiving their debtors.

And the children cried out with a burst of delight,
  For there were their parents, their sisters and
    brothers,
  And each as he lightened the sufferings of others,
Grew moment by moment more bright.

And happy the children as happy could be,
  As they turned o'er the leaves—let us hope, O
    my Friend,
  They may find in that book, ere they pause at the
    end,
A corner for you and for me.

KATY.

Look at Katy, look at Katy,
  Dancing here and there ;
Pretty simple-hearted Katy,
  With the soft brown hair.
Fears and cares and troubles weighty,
Gentle, turn aside from Katy.

Running here and running yonder,
  Careless as a child,
Deer in forest's depths that wander,
  Do not roam more wild.

Deer in ferny glades that meet her,
Have not eyes whose glance is sweeter,
  Kinder, or more mild.
Full of grace is little Katy,
  Simple as a child.

Once I sought her as a wooer,
  Thought to gain her love.
Spoke of eyes whose depths were bluer
  Than the skies above.
Spoke of lips more tender red,
Than the first moss rose, I said.
  Katy listened—clear blue eyes
  Widening with surprise,
Little mouth with pearly teeth,
Laughter—shown beneath.
  Silly Katy stayed dissembling,
Just one moment stayed by me,
  Then she turned, and sobbing, trembling,
Straight to mother's arms fled she.

" Mother, save me ! Mother, save me ! "
Safe within the parent nest,
  Little Katy turned to brave me,
Shielded on her mother's breast.

Katy's father, Katy's mother,
  Will not let their darling roam;
Little sisters, elder brothers,
  Vow to keep her safe at home.
Katy says she will not leave them,
Says she could not bear to grieve them;
  She will stay at home.
I am patient, love is great,
Hope is lingering at the gate.
  I am waiting, Katy dearie ;
Katy darling, do not fear me;
  Sweet one, I can wait.

SUMMER.

God's summer like a favoured child,
    Comes lightly through the trees ;
He gives her all her heart desires,
    Nor finds her hard to please ;
Her fleckered hair with flowers is fair,
    The grass has reached her knees.

He gives her orchards bent with fruit,
    And shady woodland bowers,
And groves alive with thrushes' notes,
    And meadows bright with flowers.
The Night and Day, her guardians they ;
    Her nymphs, the rosy Hours.

And yet, for all her queenly realm,
　　She like a child appears,
For rich and poor she runs to meet,
　　The young and bowed with years ;
Her kisses sweet bid cares retreat,
　　And bless Remorse with tears.

O hark ! her heralds call without,
　　The eager cuckoo cries,
The bees go humming tales of sweets,
　　To idle butterflies.
Beyond the gates, God's summer waits,
　　With welcome in her eyes.

THE DAY OF THE CRUCIFIXION, AS RELATED BY AN EYE-WITNESS.

I HAD been lying on my chamber floor,
My long low chamber looking towards the east,
But when the fifth hour came, I rose once more.

I washed my hands, I smooth'd my vestments
   creased,
I girt my long-fringed robe of Tyrian dye,
And wandered forth to mingle with the feast.

And from the Judgment Hall, as passing by,
I wondering paused to watch the gathering crowd,
I saw the sentenced man led out to die.

I could not see his face, his head was bowed,
Where some rude hands a cactus crown had set ;
The mocking multitude was shouting loud.

I could not hear the name they called, and yet
I caught the mingled cries of " Prophet," " King,"
As on I passed to lonely Olivet.

And near at hand a trembling, tearful thing,
A woman, met me clad in sombre brown,
Afar that sad procession following.

While further on a man came hurrying down,
Who cried in passing, " Haste to Calvary,
And see this fellow claiming Cæsar's crown."

But yet I did not turn, it seemed to me
That God's great sunshine were a fairer thing,
Than human sufferings terrible to see.

How sweet the woods were! all the air was
  spring,
Half mellowed round to summer, and the cold
That pleasant morn had taken sudden wing.

Amidst the olive's dusky greens and golds
I lingered till at last I rose dismayed,
To find the day so many more hours old.

And down the hill I hastened, sore afraid,
To risk my vows, but reached the Temple soon,
And veiled my face and knelt me down and
  prayed.

The quiet day was drawing near to noon,
When suddenly a leaden blackness fell—
Blacker than darkness—neither sun nor moon.

Then strongest terror seized me like a spell ;
I stumbled groping, tottered on my face,
And reason left me ; earth seemed turned to Hell.

How long I lay I know not ; God in grace
Suspended consciousness, and when I woke
My fear was gone ; I looked about the place.

The crowd was kneeling round me, no one spoke ;
Our eyes were down, then came a moment's hush,
And then a shrieking, maddening tempest broke.

The solid earth was shaking like a rush,
A sound like heaven's curtains rent in two,
A cry, a sense of death, a fiery flush.

And once again we looked, yet all we knew
Before that looking—veil-less, torn, and bare,
The Holiest of Holies rose in view.

A moment longer, then in mad despair
The crowd fled weeping—groaning,—as for me,
I staggered backwards down the marble stair.

The light had broke once more, the sun was
    free ;
I ran, I fled, I passed it unaware,
That wounded body hanging on a tree.

A SUPPLICATION.

" Thou fool, this night thy soul shall be required
of thee."

Not in the night, O Lord!   Not in the night,
   But in the broad daylight,
     Then claim Thy right,
  And call my soul away.
     Beneath Thy sight I know,
  Night turns to day,
    And darkness cannot stay,
  But oh!   But oh!
With us, frail things, it is not so;
Have pity on my weakness; eyes like ours
Require the sun to wake them like the flowers.

To hark,
And catch the distant singing of the lark,
To see the sunshine spreading glory wide,
To scent the lilies by the water side,
To take one look at earth in all her pride,
And so to die were death without its pain!
But, oh! the struggle in the dark,
To call for light and call in vain,
To watch the candle's tiny spark,
And moan for day again,—
To moan for day which will not come,
But in its stead the darkness of the tomb.
Oh! Lord, defend us each from such a doom,
From such a nightmare strife
Betwixt the borderlands of Life and Life.

THE ROOT'S COMPLAINT.

THE root one day complained
　To the earth, its mother dear,
How all things went towards heaven,
　Around them far and near,—
How of all her happy children,
　'Twas the only grovelling thing,
Which never mounted upward,
　Where the brown lark hangs to sing.

" The blue and distant mountains
　That stand against the sky,
The trees whose leafy banners
　Float year by year more high,

And bud and stalk and branches
　　Are mounting evermore,
Earth's thousand voices singing,
　　One glad Excelsior.

" And the children, too, grow upwards,
　　With blue eyes fixed on Heaven ;
And good men when they die,
　　Whose souls from sin are shriven,
Mount upwards—mount so far
　　They pierce beyond the sky.
Alas ! Alas ! why should it be
　　That all things rise but I ? "

But the Earth, whose heart is large
　　To hold her children's pain,
To the root gave answer back,
　　Till her words brought peace again.

"And is it such thy grief,
  Poor lonely child," she said,
" Because thou mayest not strive
  To the blue skies overhead.

"Ah ! how would the trees spring up,
  With their tall tops waving free,
Or how would the flowers awake,
  If it were not first for thee ?
From thee the fir-trees gain
  Their strength from day-to-day ;
And without thee, the violets
  Would.wither and fade away.

" For some are born to shine,
  The worship of all around,
And some to suffer alone,
  In the darkness underground.

The fresh green shoots and the blossoms,
   Towards heaven they gladly start ;
But thou, unknown, inglorious,
   Hast still the nobler part."

UNE LONGUE PATIENCE.

Oh ! it is difficult to still
The beatings of the blood, to will
And yet do nothing ; standing nigh,
To watch the empty days go by.
Blank days we feel the power to fill,
Yet may not lift a hand until.

O great Until !   O Thing to be !
We stretch forth longing arms to thee.
We cry, " Come soon, our time is small,
We lose our strength, our hope, our all ;

From this long prison set us free,
We faint before eternity."

In vain we cry with tears and prayers,
With sinking heart and chill despairs ;
The moment yet is far away,
To-morrow will not rise to-day.
In God's good time our present cares,
Shall form the crown the future wears.

PAYING BACK.

WHAT shall I give to you, my friend, my friend,
For all the treasures that you send,
The gifts and costly tokens without end?
You fill my lap with flowers, you deck my hair
With jewels bright and rare.
This diamond on my hair—O, Friend, be sure
That eastern sultans' are not half so pure,
Nor kingly Koh-i-noor ;
What shall I give you back for all you bring ?
I am so poor, so poor.

What shall you give to me, my friend, my friend,
For all the treasures that I send,
The gifts and costly tokens without end?
What shall you give to me who love you best?
O, dear! you must have guessed.
If you would show me treasures that I prize
Above all shining things in earth or skies,
Then raise for once your eyes.
If you would give me more than India's wealth,
Then let me take one little kiss by stealth
From where that diamond lies.

BYGONES.

I was thinking of him to-night by the hearth,
  My old, old love of days gone by,
And of how like a meteor he crossed my path,
  Quick to arise and quicker to die.

Thinking of him in his six-foot pride,
  With his blue-black eyes, and his blue-black
    hair,
With his air of the world I had never tried,
  And his laugh half scornful half debonair.

Is it so long since we met in the spring,
  In the old grey house on the Kentish wold,
Where we walked to hear the nightingales sing,
  And he was eager and I was cold?

He who had learned the ways of the world,
  The droop of the eyes and the low soft speech,
And I like a tendril half uncurled,
  That struggles and clings to the branch in
    reach.

Was it a thing that he cared to gain,
  The glance of worship from girlish eyes?
He who had conquered again and again,
  Why should he strive for so sorry a prize?

Little by little I opened my soul,
  Showed him all to its troublous deep;
Little by little he wakened the whole,
  Sixteen summers had held it asleep.

Up and down in the dear green wood—
　　Through the scented rose paths together we
　　　　walked,
Everything noble and pure and good,
　　Seemed to grow nearer the while he talked.

Looking up through the trellis of boughs,
　　Watching the stars as they woke in the blue,
Philomel singing her love and her vows,
　　In the rose bush hidden away from view.

Was it so strange if I opened the gate
　　Of the little still garden he first cared to claim !
Lilies were blowing in maidenly state,
　　Violets, their sweet heads were hanging for
　　　　shame.

Blossom and fragrance, summer and song,
　　Down at his feet in my fervour I cast,
" See, O my garden !　We watched for him long,
　　Take him your King and your Master at last."

Little it seemed to him, I suppose,
 That the gate should open and let him go
  through ;
Passing a lily, and plucking a rose,
 Pleasant for idling an hour or two.

Shadow for substance, gold for dross,
 Willingly bartering my truth for a lie ;
Gambler risking his all on a toss,
 Never was more of a fool than I.

Well, I forgive him, for now I know
 All that I suffered, he suffered before ;
Little white hands had dealt him the blow,
 Little false words had pierced him sore.

Something common to women and men,
 Perhaps a wound, or was it a scar ?
Roses were never so sweet since then,
 And earth's best music had notes ajar.

Judging of all by one false face,
    Reading by light of the hard blue eyes ;
Oh ! if woman can prove so base,
    How should he sever the truth from the lies !

Say, I was innocent, helpless, a child,
    Yes, and he held her guileless, too ;
Deep dark eyes may be shadowed and wild,
    But surely Heaven is mirrored in blue !

What if I spoke from a stainless breast,
    Were not her words as soft and low ?
All that I, burning for shame, confessed,
    Had she not whispered it long ago ?

Ah ! and his loss was the worst, I allow ;
    Yes, I confess it through all my tears ;
See, I can smile as I speak of him now,
    Looking back through the shadows of years.

K

Now, to-day, if we met in the street,
    I could pass him by with never a start;
Once at his name, like a host would beat,
    The warring pulses against my heart.

Yes, I am cured, as whole I think,
    As had we never met in the May,
And never walked by the water's brink,
    Nor lingered at eve in the scented hay!

Now I can fathom his wound aright,
    Now that my own had ceased to ache;
I could take his hand in my own to-night
    Without a pang for the dead year's sake.

For many a change by the sea and land,
    Must touch the earth for sorrow or weal,
And hearts may change as the shifting sand,
    And hopes may wither, and wounds may heal.

Gone is the child of those far-off days,
    With the laughing face and the rose in her
        breast,
And I stand with my feet in the great Highways,
    And I work, and wait for the evening's rest.

COMING HOME.

CAN this be what I dreamed of ?
Good people, tell me true,
Is this the quaint old village
That looks so strange and new ?
" We know not what you ask for,
Old man with hoary head,
But this is Burton township,
And a thriving place " they said.

If this be Burton township,
And yonder Burton street,
Where is the snug old alehouse
Where the guests were wont to meet ?

The signboard swung beside it,
The fires blazed warm and well,
" Five years ago they razed it,
When they built the Grand Hotel."

Down there beyond the milestone,
There stretched the village green,
The elms spread wide around it,
And the children played between,—
" The elms were felled last autumn,
For they said they stopped the air,
And the green is fenced and planted,
To make the rich man's square."

Where is the little chapel
Where we knelt each Sabbath day?
The children's ringing voices?
And the pastor kind and grey?

" When they built our fine St Mary's,
They pulled the chapel down ;
The pastor left the neighbourhood,
And our choir is sent from town. "

The little house we lived in,
It stood beside the pool,
With the thick laburnum bushes,
Where I used to hide from school ? —
" Our waterworks were finished,
When the pool began to fail ;
And the ground was cleared about it
To build the County Jail. "

If my little house is ruined,
Alas ! where then is she ?
My blue-eyed laughing Bessie,
With our child upon her knee ?

Oh ! tell me where to seek her,
The wife of Robin Dair ;
You'd know her by her bonnie eyes
And pale bright primrose hair.

" What mean you by your ravings,
Old man, we cannot say ;
But Robin's wife was stricken
When Robin went away.
They laid her in the churchyard ground
(They say for grief she died),
'Twas thirty years last Christmas,
And her child is at her side.

THE BITTER FRUIT.

"Who shall taste the bitter fruit?"
　　Cried a voice from Heaven's gate,
　　Crying early, crying late,
"Who shall taste the bitter fruit?"

Many came and many strove—
　　" Not for you," the angel said,
　　" Hangs the bitter fruit o'erhead,
Shaded in the darkling grove. "

Till at last came one whose head
  Spirit forms had crowned with bay,
  Friendly stars to guide his way,—
"Take and eat," the angel said.

Thus he gained the longed-for prize,
  Took and ate the much desired,
  And the peoples, till they tired,
Cried his praises to the skies.

Forth into the world he stept,
  Toiled with book and toiled with pen,
  Brought back many gifts for men,
Built and framed whilst others slept.

Up and down the lands he went,
  Always silent, always wise,
  Stately wisdom in his eyes,
On his brow, a sad content.

And the peoples wearied never,
  Shouted as he passed them mute,
  " He has gained the bitter fruit,
He has won renown for ever."

By his father walked a child,
  And he heard the people's cries,
  Saw the hero's listless eyes,
While the many cringed and smiled,

" Father, why this proud repute ?
  Who is this they rank so high ? "
  " Child, the whole wide world knows why,
He has gained the bitter fruit."

Then the child looked troubled sore,
  " Father, I have always said—
  " Day by day our daily bread—
Must I ask for something more ? "

Suddenly the hero turned,
    Stooped and raised him to his breast,
    " No, my child, for that is best,
Bread is sweet and lightly earned.

" One may climb, but many fall,
    I have toiled and I have striven ;
    God the promised hire has given,
But his gifts He keeps for all.

THE CHANGELING.

I HAD a baby, wee, pet grief,
A little wailing grief ;
Its little form so fair and light,
I held it in my arms all night.
I let it sob itself to rest,
Its little hands against my breast ;
To crush a bud I would as lief
As harm my baby grief.

But when I woke, the traitor thing,
Had grown a fiend, with fangs and sting,

With savage claws and horny palms,
I held a monster in my arms.
Its cruel clutch drew wounds and tears,
Its fiery fingers pricked like spears ;
It galled, it pierced, it stung me so.
Ah, me ! the pain will never go.

OUT AT NIGHT.

By Naples' Bay
At night I lay,
With earth's great heaven above me,
And the winds went by
With a lingering sigh,
As though the dear things loved me.

The stars in sight
Were scant and white,
With the first cold touch of morning,
While yet no ray
Of brightening day
From eastern cloud was dawning.

A sound of feet,
A thrill as sweet
As had some goddess past me ;
I looked, I saw
What form she bore,
What marvel bent and claspt me.

In woman's guise
With mortal eyes,
The goddess stood before me,
And clear and bright
As a summer night,
Her southern face hung o'er me.

" O eyes like stars,
With the light of Mars
And the soft blue shine of Venus;
Oh, queenly lips
Where the moonbeam dips,
Say, what can come between us ! "

I claspt her waist,
In my madman's haste
I bore her through the gloaming,
To where the sea,
In childish glee,
In slow white waves was foaming.

We reached my bark
That void and dark
Tost lightly on the billow;
I let her float,
My bonnie boat,
A maiden's lap my pillow.

How sweet I slept!
The breezes crept,
And touched my temples lightly,
The stars above
Looked down in love,
The little waves curled brightly.

But when I woke,
As daylight broke
With sullen lightning flashes,
A heap of clay
My goddess lay,
My couch but dust and ashes.

UNFULFILLED.

I AM dying, O Lord! I am dying,
  Brain fire, with my feet in the snow;
My limbs all a-tremble are lying,
  Awaiting their pitiless foe.
He comes, rushes Fever to blind me,
  A bloodhound with poisonous breath,
I hear him, his steps are behind me,
  I feel them, those fangs that are death.

The words that I utter are madness,
  The silence I keep is despair,
All whispers of hope and of gladness
  Have died as they fell through the air.

No friendship, no love, can avail me,
  No hand, but it burns on my brain,
My pulses like demons assail me,
  My strength is the slave to my pain.

All spells of religion and duty,
  All manhood and manhood's desire,
All pureness and wisdom and beauty,
  Are scorched and burned up in the fire;
And the ladder of Jacob, the dreamer,
  No longer is stretched from above,
Yet still, O my Lord! my Redeemer!
  I cling, I have root in Thy love!

I must die, like a deed unrecorded,
  Like a bud to be never a flower;
The knowledge, the truths, I have hoarded,
  Must fade like a spark in the shower;

A fragment, a blot, a negation
  For ever my life must remain.
But the spark Thou hast quenched at creation,
  O Lord ! Thou canst fire it again.

What matter whose lips shall proclaim it,
  If only the Truth shall go free ?
What recks it whose fervour shall frame it,
  The pæan forbidden to me ?
I care not, the present may scoff me,
  The Future forget my renown ;
Take, take the white garment from off me,
  And give to another my crown.

THE ROSE THORNS.

A KNIGHT rode forth with a wondrous shield,
Three bare thorns on a blood-red field;

Young and brave, and loyal and pure,
Valiant to fight, firm to endure.

A strange and an earnest knight was he.
" No kisses nor love nor mirth for me;

" For man was never for idling meant,
And suffering is better than brute content.

" I have fled the summer, for storms and snows;
I have gathered the thorns, and left the rose. "

They showed him crowns and honour and fame,
" Crowns are tinsel, and glory a name. "

They gave him a palace, wide and high;
" Earth is my house, my roof the sky."

They showed him a maiden fair as morn,
A thing so fair had ne'er been born.

" The rose is sweet as sweet can be,
But the thorns are best for a knight like me."

He pressed them close and they pierced him sore,
Long and grievous the wounds he bore.

They rankled festering day by day,
Till they stabbed his spotless life away.

The Angels took him up one morn,
And gave him roses without a thorn.

ASPIRATIONS.

Of all the fruits of thought, whose dewy birth
    The heavy world to sudden life has stirred,
How many, perhaps the noblest, fall to earth,
    And die unregistered !

How many hours the poet frets to waste,
    In stretching after stars beyond his reach,
And stumbles blindly as he treads in haste,
    The pebbles on the beach !

Or, like a butterfly, some fancy gay
   He follows, lured by beauty all too much ;
From flower to flower it flies, from spray to spray,
   And fades beneath his touch.

How many forms of fairness most divine
   The painter sees, yet cannot make his own !
How often wings of angels round him shine !
   He needs must see alone.

How many pure resolves and willing prayers,
   Unripened, unfulfilled, to darkness fall !
How many climbers faint on Jacob's stairs,
   Nor reach the gates at all !

Then let us stretch us on the easy grass,
   Content with sun and blueness of the sky ;
Though eager feet around us come and pass,
   We care not, you and I.

The free and wholesome air, the rest from strife,
   Shall be enough, my friend, for you and me;
Rejoicing in the common things of life,
   Content that such things be.

THE BALLAD OF ERNEST, SON OF THE EARL OF STRATHNEY.

Who is this who comes so stately,
  With his falchion on his wrist ?
'Tis the one we mourned so lately,
  'Tis the lord so long we miss'd.
Come, my lady, fair and cherished,
  Cast your widow's weeds away,
For the one we wept as perished,
  Strathney's lord comes home to-day.

But he waved his hand in sorrow,
  And he stopped them with a frown,
" Though I live, I die to-morrow,
  Ere the summer sun be down.

Savage Ralph is now my jailer;
  Love, we only meet to part "—
While the lady's cheek grew paler,
  He has clasped her to his heart.

" Dearest, brighter days are dawning,
  With my blood I seal the right;
Care and death may come with morning,
  Let us both be glad to night. "
Thus he spoke with brave assurance,
  On his face was nought but joy;
Father's joy and husht endurance,
  As he bent to kiss his boy.

" Ah! my Lord," said Lady Roddice,
  " Let the tyrant do his worst,
From our arms and through our bodies,
  Cruel Ralph must snatch you first. "

But he answered sternly, shorter,
  " Ere I left, I pledged my faith,
Roddice, be your father's daughter,
  Surrey's child should smile at death. "

Grave and silenced bowed the lady,
  Flushed her cheek with noble shame ;
Hand in hand through alleys shady,
  Turned they back the way she came.
Soon the place is bare and lonely,
  All have gone to hall or bower,
Blue-eyed Ernest lingers only,
  Ernest, heir of Strathney Tower.

Now across the plain he dashes,
  Swift of foot and light of limb,
Through the chilling torrent splashes,
  Up the mountain's rugged brim,

Till at last when night is falling,
  Sheer a castle stems his path,
Dogs are barking, pages calling,
  Men are drinking round the hearth.

Ralph the Marcher sits at table,
  Loud he boasts and loudly swears;
Little recks the walls of sable,
  In the gloomy room upstairs.
Strathney's lord his foe detested,
  Dies to-morrow by his hand;
On the dust his proud head rested,
  All his love locks in the sand.

Ralph is speaking, flushed, victorious,
  " Long our fray and fierce our feud;
Oh, to-morrow will be glorious,
  We shall bathe our hands in blood !

With his blood shall wash our banners,
　　Wash our outraged scutcheons white.
With all means and by all manners,
　　Let us drink success to-night."

All his hearers listening gladly,
　　Clash their glasses, beat their hands.
While their cheers are echoing madly,
　　Lo ! a boy before them stands ;—
" Cruel Ralph, my life receive it,
　　Strathney's heir and son am I.
Take the branch, the trunk, oh ! leave it,
　　In his stead I come to die. "

Ralph the Marcher beckoned scorning,
　　" Take the prisoner to the hold,
We shall see to-morrow morning
　　If this Hector's fire be cold.

Hunger, darkness, cold, and quiet,
   Often cure these hero fits ;
And I hope our prison diet,
   Soon may bring him to his wits. ''

On the morrow strongly pleading,
   Ernest once again is there ;
Ralph the Marcher little heeding,
   Seems at last to grant his prayer.
By the scaffold quietly kneeling,
   He has marked the glittering knife,
Scarcely trembles, only feeling,
   " I shall die to save his life. ''

Now a clatter in the gateway,
   And a shouting in the hall,
Then a sound of feet, and straightway
   Strathney strides amidst them all.

Knight and squire before him sweeping,
  He has claspt his child anon—
" Ah ! my boy, your mother weeping,
  Mourns her husband and her son."

" Haste ; return, oh ! comfort, tend her."
  " Father, father, let me be,
How could my weak arm defend her ?
  If I die, I set you free."
While they spoke and strove to master,
  All at once the Marcher rose.
" Sirs, behold a strange disaster,
  Conquered I, by conquered foes.

" Let our feud be settled rather ;
  From to day our quarrel ends.
Such a son and such a father,
  Needs must make the noblest friends.

Good my lord, forgive my madness ;
　Friend, forget my purpose wild.
So this day begun with sadness,
　Let it leave us reconciled. "

ON A FRIEND'S BIRTHDAY.

Now morning mists have vanished quite,
And you have reached that centre height,
Whence man can see from where he stands
The slopings paths to other lands.
The land of birth from which we came,
The land of death to which we go—
And are they different or the same?
Or near or distant?   Who can know?

Enough ! we will not prate to-day,
Of life, of death, of time, decay,
Poor used up terms whose power is gone,
Like that long mourner " overworn"—

In olden days when Chaucer sung,
Ideas were fresh, the times were young,
Then words arose from thought alone,
They held their meaning all their own,
But now like coins debas'd and old,
What use those battered bits of gold !

On that March morning long ago,
How strange to wake from rest more deep,
Than that which nightly lays us low,
And blinds our eyes and cheats us so—
That weird intoxication sleep—
And then unknowingly to lie,
And grow through helpless hours and days,
And learn by most uncertain ways,
Your new, perplext identity,
Till somehow (Ah, the How and Why
Are distant from us as the sky,)
Your powers grew wide, your strength of brain,

M 2

And spread and flourished hour by hour,
And blossomed to a perfect flower—
And like a flower it waits to wane,
Through many a snare your feet have passed,
Through much to darken, much to try,
And many a doubt you've crush'd at last,
And many a phantom forced to fly,
And dived beneath the surface lie,
And snatched the truth and held it fast,
But never pierced through years of strife,
That deepest, darkest mystery—Life.

TOO LATE.

SHE died with my arms around her,
   And her hand in my own firm claspt,
And my only thought was a blessing,
   That her trouble was over at last.

She who had suffered so wildly,
   Suffered and cried in her pain,
Worked when her heart was breaking,
   Prayed when she knew it was vain.

There she lay in her chamber,
  Cold and quiet and still,
Trampled and crushed and broken,
  Now let her rest her fill.

I had caught her breath as it left her,
  I had folded her hands at rest,
And had placed the rose as she asked me
  With the letters against her breast.

And then as she lay in the silence,
  I saw with a sob and a cry,
How the face had changed in a moment,
  To the face of the days gone by.

The pain and the lines had left it,
  And the sweet, sweet lips had a smile,
And the eyes that had ached for weeping,
  Were closed for a long, long while.

When first I stood in the doorway,
  She had stretched her arms out wide,
And cried that her prayer was answered,
  And we kissed before she died.

O God! my worship, my darling!
  That it ever should come to this,
Severed by years of torment,
  And joined by the breadth of a kiss.

I took her head on my bosom,
  Mine, mine when having was vain,
But I never wished for a moment,
  She might live her days over again.

PASSING AWAY.

WE laid her down to rest at eve,
  She looked so smooth and fair,
We never guessed that flesh and life
  So nearly severed were.

The sun from out the purple west
  Was shining warm and bright :
It played about her wasted cheek,
  And tinged her eyes with light.

Her children stood beside her couch,
  Her babe was on her knee ;
Kate's little face was grave and sad,
  But Willie prattled free.

'Twas, " Mother, I have worked all day,
  And pulled up all the weeds ;
And sister Kate has helped as well,
  To rake and sow the seeds.

" And, mother, puss has killed a bird,
  It lay all stiff and bare,
But Kate and I have made a grave,
  And buried birdie there."

She stoopt and kissed his eager face,
  " Enough, my little son,
Your work to-day was rightly meant,
  And it was bravely done."

Then Alice touched the well-loved notes,
    And sang the prophet's song—
" The Lord himself my Shepherd is,
    He leadeth me along."

She sang it over line by line;
    I thought I ne'er should hear
A strain again so heavenly sweet,
    A voice so full and clear.

" Though through the Vale of Death I go,
    Yet still I know no fears,
Thy rod and staff shall comfort me,"
    We could not hold our tears.

But when we turned, her face was white
    As hawthorn's bloom in May ;
Her head against the pillows leant,
    As one asleep she lay.

Her hands were claspt as though she prayed,
  A smile was on her lips;
The setting sun had left her face,
  And kissed her finger tips.

The little children round her couch,
  Stood hushed in silence deep,
To think of streams and pastures green,
  The Shepherd and the sheep.

We took the baby from her knee,
  The children from her side;
The setting sun it did not die,
  More gently than she died.

DAISY'S THISTLE.

WE were walking in the meadows,
  My wife Kathleen and I,
Adown the pleasant pastures,
  Where the sheep were grazing nigh.

And there our little Daisy
  Was sitting in the grass,
So deep in childish musings,
  She did not hear us pass.

We stood beneath the beeches,
 And watched our child that day,
The sweetest little maiden,
 That ever bloomed in May.

But now her eyes were tearful,
 Her little face was stoopt,
Above a great red thistle,
 That hung its head and droopt.

" Indeed, poor pretty thistle,"
 We heard our darling say,
" We all are very sorry,
 To watch you fade away.

" And I would give my largest doll,
 My spade and puzzles three,
To bring you back again to life,
 But yet it must not be.

" For listen, queenly thistle,
  Bend down your purple head,
And I will tell to comfort you
  What James the gardener said.

" He said that if we left you,
  Your feathered seeds would fly,
And plant the grass with prickles,
  And choke it by-and-by.

" But if in might he crushed you,
  And struck your beauty low;
The fields would bloom and flourish,
  The sheep would feed and grow.

" And so, poor pretty thistle,
  Your life a gift will be,
To die for others' good, as once
  The Saviour died for me."

We waited not to hear her more,
   But softly turned away,
And left our little darling,
   To have her own sweet say.

SONNET.

LORD, day by day, without Thy barrier door
I stand and call, " Open, Good Master, wide,
Behold how long I wait and kneel outside ;
My hands are heavy and my feet are sore,
How long, oh ! how much longer must I wait ? "
So called I, chafing at that fast closed gate.
When straight the Master's voice made answer
    back :
" Who calls my coming, slow ; my promise,
    slack ?

Each morn and every evening at my door
I hear you knock, and haste to let you in ;
I haste, yet find you wandered back once more—
Back to the world, its folly and its sin.
Like Pilate, asking what you do not heed,
Unanswered turn you back, unblessed, unfreed."

POEMS,

WRITTEN FROM FOURTEEN TO SEVENTEEN INCLUSIVE.

SONNET.

THERE are some faces which a smile lights up
Like sparkling nectar in a crystal cup ;
And though without a beauty of its own,
A face an artist would think scorn to paint,
Yet from the glory of that smile alone,
Grows radiant as the features of a saint ;
As if the fragrant white-robed soul within,
Decked in the beauty of her holiness,
Looked from her hiding-place all pure from
    sin,
And showed more beauty since her mask had
    less.

All earth is beauteous ; all her forms declare
That, midst the gloomiest, loveliness is there ;
But smiles which give the face another birth,
Are little less than heaven come down to earth.

AMONGST FRIENDS.

Yes, I am very happy here,
I needs must be ; with loved ones near,
We laugh and talk, we dance and sing,
And gladness holds no secret sting ;
The merry days fly smoothly o'er,
But, oh ! to be alone once more,
    Only to be alone !

I cannot think, I cannot write,
Almost I cannot sleep at night,
For voices call from hall and stair,
And footsteps echo everywhere ;

Bright faces throng the useless door,
But, oh ! to be alone once more,
   Only to be alone !

I know no quiet unminded place,
Where I might hide a little space,
To rest my heart from cares and fears,
Or cleanse perhaps with healing tears ;
I scarce have felt the want before,
But, oh ! to be alone once more,
   Only to be alone !

Well, I must learn to be content,
And lonely hours are idly spent ;
And helping hands are nobler far
Than useless, listless dreamings are ;
Such dreams are folly to the core.
But, oh ! to be alone once more,
   Only to be alone.

A CARELESS GIFT.

Not long ago, a year gone by,
  In glorious days of June,
I stood beneath the summer sky,
  And thought, " He cometh soon."

The broad green trees were full of leaf,
  The fields with flowers were gay ;
For earth had doffed her garb of grief,
  To share my joy that day.

He came—and spread where fell his look
  A sunshine through the trees ;
His voice lent music to the brook,
  And incense to the breeze.

I could not take his hand to press,
 And thank him for his light;
He did not know my helplessness,
 He had not felt his might.

And when to each he gave in sport
 A crimson-bosomed rose,
He did not guess, he never thought,
 What chanced to one of those.

THE UNSPOKEN NAME.

THERE is a little word I may not speak,
A word which children shout at cottage doors,
Which all are using still, or once have used.
For me alone that sacred word is dumb,
Yet buried in my heart it somewhere lies,
Pressed far away from petty hopes and cares.
The purest, truest thoughts, the noblest deeds,
The best from pillaged battle-fields of life,
I, day by day, have raised to guard that shrine,
Have raised to guard that little silent shrine
From earth, its passions and its frailties.
And sometimes when my soul is moved to see,

How father's kisses bend to daughter's lips,
To hear the children call their father's name,
Or watch them walk safe guarded by his side ;
Then through the gnawings of my loneliness,
A pale, bright face comes gleaming through the
      gloom,
A mighty form seems beckoning me to rise,
And nearer still the calm face stoops to mine,
And closer still the blue eyes read my own,
And smiles of pity spread from lip to brow,
Where clustering locks of falling chestnut hair,
Hang like a veil to screen the shadowy dead ;
And even as I gaze, I grieve no more ;
The widening brightness of an angel's love,
Has filled my soul and left no room for tears.

Go children, happy in a father's care,
Go place the wonted arm about his neck,
And tend him with a thousand tender deeds ;
I would not change your brighter lot for mine.

Your father is but mortal, he must die,
But him I carry always in my heart,
As very part and parcel of myself;
Him, whom I knew not while he yet was mine,
Still never leaves me through the longest years.
A parent's eyes will surely watch my ways,
To guard my footsteps even unto death,
Then greet with sinless lips his child in Heaven.

TREACHERY.

SHE stood by the window,
   A rose in her hair ;
He came in so softly
   She was not aware.
Oh ! Alice, be careful ;
   Sweet Alice, take care.

She sang half a song,
   And she sighed half in shame ;
The song was unfinished,
   Unspoken the name ;
The sigh which came after,
   Say, wherefore it came ?

He stole to the window,
  So still and so meek,
He crept up behind her,
  No word did he speak,
But he stamped in a moment
  A kiss on her cheek.

SONNET.

As when a boy whose voice has charmed his life
With sweet glad airs and thrilling strains of
    song,
What time long years have dragged their terms
    along,
And childhood's joys have turned to nobler strife,
Finds on a sudden how that voice is lost,
And how the notes that used to rise so clear,
Now fall untuned and deadened on the ear,
Like flowers before the first November frost ;

So stand I on the brink of things to come,
And see my days of childish song are fled.
And yet no nobler voice of after years
Which time will bring to take away my fears,
Has come to dry my tears for what is dead,
But like a mateless dove so wait I hush't and
    dumb.

THE CLUE.

I STOOD beneath the castle,
  In the sinking August sun,
The blaze was full on the windows,
  As I watched them every one.

And which is my loved one's casement ?
  And where does she sit and dream ?
And can she see me watching
  From my station across the stream ?

Up yonder a cage is swinging
   Within the oriel wide,
I can hear the plaintive singing
   Of the captive bird inside.

The silken draperies tremble
   In the breeze the sunset brings ;
Who sits in the shaded chamber,
   And whose is the bird that sings ?

That is my Lady's casement,
   And yonder is the Earl's,
I have caught unwatched-for glimpses
   Of the dark head's clustering curls.

But where is the bright-haired daughter,
   With the white brows, pure and wise,
With the lips whose smiles have voices,
   And the sweet and trustful eyes ?

Far up in that distant turret
  A little window shines,
The ivy has grown around it,
  And the jessamine creeps and twines.

In the box on the narrow casement
  A belt of flowers I see ;
The breeze has stol'n their perfume,
  And borne the prize to me.

Those flowers have the selfsame fragrance
  That scent of mignonette,
As the sprig we plucked together
  On the day when first we met.

Oh! that slender thread of perfume,
  Like the clue to Theseus given,
Has led me from the darksome cave
  To the warm blue gates of Heaven.

For nation speaks with nation
    Through a wire both frail and fine,
And that thread is all sufficient
    To join her heart with mine.

IFS.

If I were a painter,
  What would I seek?
The dawning blush
  On a maiden's cheek.

If I were a poet,
  What would I praise?
The innocent light,
  Of a young girl's gaze.

If I were a brother,
  What would I take ?
One golden curl
  For the old year's sake.

If I were a lover,
  What would I claim ?
A kiss from the lips
  Too dear to name.

If I were a pirate
  What would I steal ?
One priceless heart,
  For woe or for weal.

A HIDDEN LIFE.

I HAVE a life within my breast,
Which none can trouble or molest ;
Which none can see and none can know,
So very deep it lies below.

And like some beauteous fairy-land,
A city all at my command,
A place where spirits wander free,
Is this my paradise to me.

There stand the glories of the earth,
The things most prized and most of worth,
From Greece, from Rome, from every strand,
I brought them to my fairy-land.

The fairest treasures art can show,
The sweetest music heard below,
And poetry softer than the breeze,
Or wilder than the tossing trees.

There move great heroes long since dead,
Who for their country's fame have bled;
The wisest and the best of yore,
All in my soul alive once more.

There great and noble deeds are done,
There strifes are waged and battles won,
There genius triumphs over might,
And evil bows before the right.

And there when tired of things without,
When weary of the world about,
I close the gates to all around,
And enter in the enchanted ground.

Within shut out from grief and pain,
I hold with spirits my domain;
The crowd may press, I do not care,
For none but I may enter there.

WHAT SHOULD BE.

How beautiful life is while yet we're young!
How sweet to play earth's summer flowers among,
And bask in love around our pathway flung,
While earth gives all that earth can ever give,
　　　　How sweet to live!

And thus the warm blood mantling o'er my face,
I sit and ponder on the human race,
And think this earth a very pleasant place,
Yet dimly feel I have not yet the might
　　　　Of judging right.

I think of good remaining to be done,
Of noble deeds set forward one by one ;
And progress carried on from sire to son,
Till all the future turns, with tints untold,
     One blaze of gold.

I dream of climbing upward round by round
Above the mortals struggling on the ground ;
Up the bright ladder with the world's renowned,
And step by step advancing o'er the whole
     To reach my goal.

Oh ! vain delusion born of ignorance,
Shall I, so weak, where others fall, advance ?
Or do I hope to gain my end by chance ?
 Shall I obtain, when brave men shrink and
   flee,
     The victory ?

I will not strive for blessings of a day,
When life and time are fleeting fast away ;
Still ever working let me ever pray,
" Life is so short, Lord, let me do thy will,
      And then be still."

" Oh ! do not let me yearn for power or fame,
Let me be changed and yet remain the same ;
Make me more worthy of a Christian's name ;
Through life, through death, let all my object be
      To love but Thee."

SONNET.

THE blind man scarce believes us when we say
   How beauteous is the world in which we dwell.
He hears of purple night and glowing day,
   Of glorious sights of meadow, field, and fell;
And smiles maybe a poor sad smile of doubt,
" This world is not so fair as fools make out.
I do not understand—I cannot see—
What *is* this beauty?   One wide blank to me."
Poor doubter, could the scales fall off your eyes,
Then all the world would be one Paradise.
So we who live below and cannot see,
Scoff at the brightness of heaven's purity;
Not till we greet our home with opened eyes,
Shall we believe the glory of the skies.

FAIRLIGHT GLEN.

WE sat together she and I,
 She held the brush and I the pen ;
And laughingly we two did vie,
 To paint the scenes of Fairlight Glen.

I sang of fields of golden furze,
 Of blue seas stretching far away—
With one long sweeping stroke of hers,
 She pictured all I strove to say.

I told of reach of glittering beach,
   Of faint white clouds and summer skies ;
But with a touch she did as much,
   And placed it all before my eyes.

Then angered sore in mimic war,
   I seized and rent the painted sheet,
And ere her hand could bid me stand,
   It lay in ruins at her feet.

She seized my lines with flashing eyes,
   She tore them from the open book,
And turning round in wrathful guise,
   She threw them trampled in the brook.

Then laughing at our childish spleen,
   I kissed her temples flushing warm,
" The fruit we took so long to glean,
   Is ruined by a moment's storm. "

RAPHAEL'S PENANCE.

Ah ! well, I must not murmur,
  To see my painting torn,
Before to-morrow's sunset
  A fairer may be born ;
But my beauteous one, my dearest,
  For ever thence is gone.

I knew that I was sinning,
  When for Mary's sainted face,
I placed my Bianca's image,
  With brows of queenly grace ;
Yet I almost thought her worthy,
  To fill our Lady's place.

P

So I went on gladly, gladly,
  How fast the colours grew !
And I thought how doubly happy
  In one to join the two ;
To greet our Lady, Bianca,
  And yet to kneel to you.

And thus the work went forward,
  Till bright the forms had grown,
And the Virgin with her Infant,
  Looked smiling from their throne ;
But I thought no more of Mary,
  For my thoughts were all your own.

One day beside my easel,
  A snow-white Angel drew,
His wings were like the snow-drops,
  All sparkling in the dew,
And mournfully and kindly,
  His soft eyes looked me through.

But I started back in terror,
  And my soul went forth in sighs,
For I knew my guilty action,
  Had reached the sorrowing skies ;
So I shrank a conscious traitor
  Beneath those tender eyes.

And he raised his hand above me,
  His clear voice reached my ear,
And he spake in tones so thrilling,
  I could not choose but hear,
Though my heart was beating, beating,
  And my brain swam round with fear.

" Oh ! you most highly gifted,
  Oh ! most unworthy son,
Ten talents were your portion,
  While others had but one,
Yet the work you did is poorer
  Than those most poor have done.

Oh ! most unblessed, you lifted,
A lost soul like your own,
To reign in threefold glory
On our Lady's holy throne,
And placed your short-lived idol,
Where Mary rules alone.

Poor soul, your sin is grievous,
But mercy dwells on high,
And though no earthly penance,
Can cleanse it of its dye,
Yet now perform my bidding,
And sovereign help is nigh.

You must take your treasured painting,
The grandest of your art,
And with those hands that formed it,
You must rend it part by part;
So take your darling idol,
And tear her from your heart.

And I turned at last to answer,
  To beg, to pray for grace,
But the Angel form had vanished,
  And I found but empty space ;
So I rose to go in sorrow,
  And left the haunted place.

And all that dreary evening,
  And all that sleepless night,
I lay before the altar,
  And I prayed for heavenly light ;
For was she not my darling,
  My worship, my delight ?

But I rose up in the morning,
  And from that altar came,
And I kissed her pictured features
  With a love I could not tame ;
Then I tore the glowing canvas,
  And cast it in the flame.

On, onward to the village,
  Where the soft blue lake lay clear,
Where Bianca sat beside it,
  With the waters murmuring near;
So I kissed her cold white temples,
  And went without a tear.

And my useless tools beside me,
  I sat that lonely even,
When the vesper bells were ringing,
  And the cattle homeward driven,
But my eyes were full of tear-drops,
  And I felt my sin forgiven.

CLOUDLAND.

WELL, you say true,
I do live in the clouds;
  Not in the glory of the sky,
  I may not venture up so high,
  Alas! it were in vain to try,
But somewhere poised between the two,
     Up in the clouds.

Sweet fairies sail in middle air,
And tender angels pure and fair,

The spirits of the mighty dead,
Float in the brightness overhead.
A thousand whispered voices tell
Of noble hero deeds of yore,
And scattered scraps of minstrel lore,
And thoughts of summer days no more,
Arise my dreamy eyes before,
And fill my cloudy cell ;
While through those hazy walls of rain,
The shadows come and go again,
And thus when I am left alone,
I rule a dreamland all my own.
Sometimes my brain is torn and driven
By angry storms I cannot still,
That drag me with them worlds from heaven,
And toss and turn me at their will ;
Then leave me shipwrecked on the ground,
The while my throne in showers is scattered
round.

What matter? Soon the storm is past,
The soft white vapours gather fast
Tall phantom forms my cell prepare,
And silent spirits waft me there.
Ah! well. I speak no fabled lore,
A thousand souls have known before,
Ere life's first dreams and hopes were o'er.
That misty world I trow—
Have felt how dear the bower they raise,
Far from the world and all its ways—
The sanctuary, the highly prized,
The outer world idealized—
A thousand feel it now.

All ye who sometimes from the stream
Of busy life draw back to dream,
And pass, maybe, a wasted hour
'Neath suns that bring no bud to flower;
All ye whose hearts still throb and beat,
Whose pulses glow with youthful heat,

I summon all to mount with me,
To yon pale depths of mystery,
    Up in the clouds

Gladly the early morning light
Shines on those fields of gold,
And heights of glory lost to sight,
Yon temple's walls uphold.
Yet soon the sun will grow to power,
And chase the clouds away,
And we who lack aerial bower
On earth perforce must stay.
How shall we live, poor helpless things,
Longing to fly, yet clipped of wings?
Oh! weary hours we fear you not,
We will not own your sway,
For we can bear our lowly lot,
And raise it all we may.
For us perhaps some little space,
Some holier brighter resting-place,

The while kind Heaven may prepare,
And angels' pinions waft us there,
Somewhere above, we ask not where ;
Somewhere athwart those realms of air,
  Somewhere beyond the Clouds.

ON THE DEATH OF A FRIEND.

How strange the first sad morning broke,
How slow and heavily I woke,
And felt, though yet unconscious why,
A cloud had gathered o'er the sky !

Next, stealing wide my soul across,
There came the gnawing sense of loss ;
And then the truth rushed fierce and fast,
" All earthly hope is gone at last."

No more to haste with doubting feet,
To hear the worst when first we meet,
And ere we catch the slow replies,
To learn them from each other's eyes.

No more to hear the tidings read,
" He may revive, he is not dead."
And leave him, eased from full despair,
Beneath the Great Physician's care.

No more to bear from place to place,
His name before the Throne of Grace,
"To raise him in the arms of Prayer,"
And lay the sufferer gently there,

And now when all our hope has died,
Our dearest wishes been denied,
We stand with folded arms and say,
" How vain it is to hope and pray ! "

And yet I think if we could gain
One hour to see him once again,
His spirit poised on angels' wings,
Would teach us strangely different things.

All faint and wounded and alone,
We laid him at the Saviour's Throne,
But Death with stronger hand than ours,
Has led him glorious, crowned with flowers.

We bore him there with tears and dread,
While stretched unconscious on his bed ;
Death, whom we strove to thrust aside,
Has robed him in a conqueror's pride.

We asked with us he might remain,
To taste the wells of life again,
But Death, who seemed to stop their course,
Has brought him to their inmost source.

Oh ! when we think of all his bliss,
And learn such perfect love as this,
Our love in turn must needs be stirred ;
We needs must own our prayer was heard.

THE MAIDEN OF THE HILL.

CENTURIES back in the olden time,
A maiden dwelt in a distant clime,
A high blue hill was the maiden's bower,
And her hair, which fell in a glittering shower,
Was the only roof which covered her head,
From summer and winter and hailstorms dread.
So she dwelt alone that matchless queen,
Her eyes were clear and her brow serene,
Fairer she was than a child of earth,
The great Minerva had watched her birth,
While all the Olympic host had striven,
To mould in glory the darling of heaven.

And for the love of that maiden's name,
Wooers from every land there came,
For the one, the worthiest and the best,
Should lie in her bosom and share her rest.

The wind came whistling across the sea,
And he said, " Sweet maiden, roam with me.
My power is supreme and my voice is strong,
The pine trees bend as I dance along.
I can shake the earth, I can rouse the deep,
I can drive the clouds like frightened sheep,
I can change the hills to flames of blood,
And the lingering stream to a raging flood;
My mother the air, and my child the rain,
I govern the earth and I guide the main ;
And yet I can move so light, so light,
You would scarcely hear my call at night ;
I would lie in your arms so meek, so meek,
You would scarcely feel me kiss your cheek."

Q

But his words were hushed by her glance of
    pride,
And she raised her voice as she turned aside;
" I have heard the shouts from sinking ships,
And the last long cries from drowning lips;
Your power may be great, and your weapons
    strong,
But you use your might for cruel wrong."

Then the sun looked down in the maiden's
    face,
And he reined his steeds in his headlong pace,
" Come, loved one, come to the great blue sky ;
Come sit with me in my chariot high,
We will haste by day through the paths of
    light,
And bathe in the ocean's depths at night.
We will chase the moon, we will drive the
    stars,
We will pierce the night of prison bars ;

We will wake the buds with a kiss and a
   smile,
And the grateful earth shall bless the while ;
O'er lands untold you shall reign the queen,
And the flowers shall start where our steps have
   been.
Oh ! come with me for my paths are fair,
Who strides like me through the tottering air ?
The scornful wind and his child the rain,
Can never before my face remain.
I draw the streams from their deepest hold,
I freight the ears with their wealth of gold,
I visit the plum on the garden wall,
Till giddy with praise it is ripe to fall,
I whisper of love to the peach at its side,
Till it blushes and reddens and swells with
   pride."

But the maiden spoke in her cold, proud tone,
Till the sun's bright face had paler grown,

Till he turned and fled those taunting lips,
And covered his head in foul eclipse.
" Truly," she said, "your smiles are bright,
You chase before you clouds and night,
Your wanton kisses awake the flowers,
And call the buds from their opening bowers ;
You ripen the peach with your friendly heat,
And the daisies spring beneath your feet ;
Wherever you go, wherever you smile,
The earth is fruitful—a little while ;
But woe to the plant whate'er its dower,
Which lives alone in the light you shower ;
The kisses it thought so sweet before,
Will wither and scorch ere the year be o'er,
And the warmth and light which gave it birth,
Will strike it dead to the panting earth."

Then the sea whose voices are never still,
Came groaning and tossing around the hill,
" Forsake, beloved one, your island hold,

The cliffs are bleak and the earth is cold,

Through all the world there is none like me,

Come leap to the arms of the matchless sea.

You shall have for subjects all that swims,

And the soft seaweed shall rest your limbs;

The mermaids pale shall your whims attend,

And the laughing Naïad shall be your friend.

From east to west, from south to north,

The mighty rivers go rushing forth,

Their waves are strong and their waves are
    high,

They nourish the earth as they thunder by,

And town and village around them rise,

That owe their life to the stream they prize.

Their flowers and fruit to the river king,

As festive offerings the people bring ;

While others, their hands besmeared with blood,

Toss their babes to the hungry flood.

But for all their pride, and their honours vain,

They are less to me than the drops of rain ;

Their march of triumph must soon be past,
And they all must reach my gates at last;
They tremble and faint when they think of me,
For they know their fate when they reach the sea.

The gentle streams and the truant brooks
Come shyly forth from their mountain nooks;
Through meadow and marsh they silent wend,
And the young things sigh to reach the end:
For they hate the toil through the stubborn
    ground,
And the hard stiff banks which hold them round;
And they long for the freedom, the peace, and
    rest,
They will find at last on their father's breast."

But the maiden spoke with a flush on her
    cheek,
" The rivers must die and the springs are
    weak;

Yet I hold the least as worthier far
Than you, O sea, in your glories are.
The grass and the corn and the forest flower,
All owe their life to the river's power;
And the fields whose tints are always bright,
Are fed by the brooklets day and night,
For there is not a flood howe'er unblest,
But has lent its strength to aid the rest ;
There is not a stream however small,
But has given its little—perhaps its all.
But you have wasted your matchless might,
Or used it only to blast and blight.
You dim the earth with your poisonous breath,
And your touch would doom the flowers to
    death ;
No grass will grow where your waves have
    rolled,
No corn will rustle its lengths of gold ;
But you toss for ever a world disgraced,
A salt accursed and barren waste."

Then there fell on all a speechless fear,
And heaven and earth were hushed to hear,
For neither the wind nor the sun nor the sea,
Could guess who the maiden's choice should
    be.

Like a fair white lily she bent to the ground,
And there where an unseen violet grew,
The delicate stalk she snapped in two ;
And first to her lips and then to her breast,
Its quivering dew-stained leaves she prest.

" Behold, oh ! wind and sun and sea,
Whom I have chosen my love to be.
I have searched the world from pole to pole,
But I have not found a kindred soul ;
I have searched the world from east to west,
And I find I love the violet best."

A POET'S FEAR.

Oh ! heavy is the gift I bear,
At once a blessing and a care,
A thing for gratitude and prayer.

Like some tall ship that lacks the hand
To guide it to the distant land,
Helmless and captainless I stand.

And when I think how fair the freight,
I tremble for the vessel's fate,
And moan—" The gift is all too great."

Oh! can she breast the homeward breeze,
When all her decks are filled like these?
Or will she sink in middle seas?

Although I ill can guard my trust,
Yet do my best I will and must;
I may not let the treasure rust.

The captain's choice has heaped the deck,
His care will shield his own from wreck,
And hold the struggling helm in check.

And he who chose me helpless quite,
The ship to bear his cargo bright,
Will teach me how to bear it right.

POEMS OF CHILDHOOD.

WRITTEN FROM NINE TO THIRTEEN INCLUSIVE.

A REVERIE.

I LOVE to linger in this spot,
Where nature is, and man is not ;
I would that it had been my lot,
   To live and labour here.

Within this wild unchristened dell,
From out the rock I'd carve my cell,
And here in peaceful bliss I'd dwell,
   With no disturbers near.

I am alone, yet not alone ;
The harebell calls this vale her own,
And foxgloves tall themselves have sown
    The ancient rocks between.

And here is seen the poppy red,
And here the violet shows her head,
So hidden in her leafy bed,
    That she can scarce be seen.

The lark is soaring far above,
Singing her song of joy and love,
The bee is buzzing in the grove ;
    I love them all full well.

Can I have better company
Than these poor birds so full of glee ?
Yes, there is one more dear to me,
    My darling Isabel.

You are so firm and I so weak,
I am so wild and you so meek,
I cannot of your praises speak ;
    Too many they to tell.

My cottage home is dull and dreary,
And I feel lone and I feel weary,
Without herself to keep me cheery ;
    Come, come, my Isabel.

MY LITTLE GARDEN.

I HAVE a little garden,
  Which is my very own,
And flowers grow and blossom there,
  Which my own hands have sown.

I've cared for them and watered them
  With my little watering-pot,
And dug and raked and hoed the soil,
  When the summer sun was hot.

It is my pride and my delight
   That little spot of ground,
And the air is fragrant with the scent
   Of flowers that bloom around.

Every morning out I go,
   And with unceasing care,
I, from my pretty garden take,
   The sweetest flowers there.

And running to my mother's room,
   I lay them near her head;
And when she wakes she knows she'll find
   The flowers upon her bed.

The autumn winds are blowing,
   The year is fleeting by,
And all my pretty flowers,
   Must wither soon and die.

R

But after they are dead,
  Their memory will remain,
Like the grateful hues of nature,
  After a shower of rain.

And when the bright springtide returns,
  New and fresher flowers will bloom ;
Then I'll no longer mourn for those
  Fair blossoms in their tomb.

THE NIGHT WATCH.

Oh! it was a dreary night,
With no moon or stars so bright,
To shed on me their kindly light,
   Watching for my Katie.

I sat still and ever still,
Resting on the window sill,
With eye turned towards the distant hill,
   Traversed by my Katie.

I sat there till very late,
Watching for my chosen mate,
Watching for my darling Kate,
   Waiting for my Katie.

I waited long and anxiously,
I waited all impatiently,
For a darling girl was she,
   My loved and cherished Katie.

It was long past time for her to return,
For she had set off in the early morn,
To go to the town to buy a new churn,
   And quickly walked my Katie.

I watched till 'twas day again,
And distracted seemed my brain,
When I thought with bitter pain,
   I ne'er more should see my Katie.

I went out in the early dawn,
I went out in the dewy morn,
I went out on the way to town,
  Searching for my Katie.

I went o'er the ground again and again,
But, alas! 'twas all in vain,
And half-crazy home I came,
  Mourning for my Katie.

I summoned all the labourers about,
From their houses I called them out,
And prayed of them to make a rout,
  And find my darling Katie.

At length, oh, sorrow! she was found
Lying dead upon the ground,
She had been killed by a bloodhound,
  Oh! cruel death for Katie.

Our bodies two, our hearts were one,
My earthly joy has been undone,
And I will ever live alone,
  Weeping for my Katie.

SUNSET.

Sun, dear sun, a little longer,
Linger o'er the corn-fields yonder,
  With your brilliant yellow light,
  Ever warm and ever bright.

See, he's sinking, sinking fast,
Every glimmer seems the last ;
  Ah ! we can just see him still,
  Half hidden by the lofty hill.

Many clouds are floating o'er him,
Dancing to and fro before him,
  But he struggles bravely on,
  He will not hastily be gone.

See his face like fire is red,
And he shakes his haughty head,
  With a gesture stern and proud,
  And soon hath vanished every cloud.

But his reign is nearly o'er,
And death is knocking at his door;
  See, he trembles, sore afraid,
  Half in light and half in shade.

There now he's touched the mountain top,
And there a moment he doth stop;
  But the pale moon is gliding on,
  He quivers, trembles, and is gone.

A DREAM.

WITH fever torn, with grief opprest,
Last night I laid me down to rest,
But sleep, alas! was far away,
Tossing and moaning low I lay;
And when sleep soothed my aching brow,
I dreamt a dream which haunts me now.
Methought I stood upon a plain,
The wind howled fierce, fast fell the rain;
The sea below was dashing high,
And lightning flashes lit the sky;
Sudden before my wondering sight,
There stood an angel black as night.

He held three balls of vivid flame,
Sin, Death, and Judgment, they by name.
He threw them laughing in my hand,
To be to me a burning brand ;
And then with mocking scorn he fled,
And left me filled with awful dread.
To cast away those balls of fire,
Such was my wild my mad desire,
I threw them into the foaming sea ;
Angry, she tossed them back to me.
I cast them up into the air,
But it hearkened not to my despair,
For it threw them back to me again.
With a gust of wind that shook the plain,
I buried them deep beneath the sod,
But cruel Pluto, Hell's dark God,
Cast them up with a hideous yell,
That came from the uttermost depths of Hell.
Despairing now, with fury worn,
I cursed the day when I was born.

"Would that the lightning might strike me low,"
I cried aloud in my depth of woe ;
"Would that the Earth might open wide,
And let me deep in darkness hide."
Filled with affliction, pain, and wrath,
I drew a glittering dagger forth,
But as it touched my heaving breast,
I woke from out my troubled rest.

TIME'S UP.

THE soldier weary of his rounds,
Fast keeping watch on foemen's grounds,
How sweet to him the signal sounds,
            Time's up!

The rebel kneeling at his prayer,
With bandaged eyes and forehead bare,
To him how harsh the words declare,
            Time's up!

The wife who bade her James farewell,
As on the steamer's deck she fell,
The words came like a dying knell,
$\qquad$ Time's up.

The prisoner weary of his chain,
Condemned to years of labour vain,
It came to him to ease his pain,
$\qquad$ Time's up.

The sailors resting on the beach,
With gold and wine a store for each,
How stern to them the boatswain's screech,
$\qquad$ Time's up !

The schoolboys tired of school and Greek,
All eager for some boyish freak,
No more will hear their master speak,
$\qquad$ Time's up.

The wounded soldiers home on leave,
They must the same stern words receive,
Though wives despair and dear ones grieve,
Time's up.

The negro bent with aching brain,
To cut the tough-barked sugar cane,
Those words bring life to him again,
Time's up.

And so to each that voice must sound,
Though buried deep to all around,
The echoes of our hearts resound,
Time's up.

Although our life be glad and gay,
That voice will come to us some day,
Death knocking at the door will say,
Time's up.

THE EXHIBITION.

In old Tradition's days of health and youth,
When heroes warred and wandered after truth,
When glorious deeds were done and tales were
    told,
All in the spring-time ere men's hearts grew old,
Then there uprose a wild rebellious man,
Striving to do what never mortal can,
To form the lifeless, senseless clay from out,
One who should breathe and speak and move
    about.
His boast through half the world he thundered
    forth;
They heard—the patient gods—they heard in
    wrath,

"Down with the man who would with gods
    compete,
Who with one stroke could lay him at their feet."
The gods he mocked uprose in anger sore,
For never man had crossed their will before.
Stern Perseus seized that fierce Medusa's head,
The which if mortal look on he is dead.
And Vulcan from his mountain caverns came,
And drear-eyed Pluto from his haunts of flame ;
Flew rosy Cupid with his poisoned dart,
To strike the death-blow to the foeman's heart.
A thousand gods uprose with one accord,
And stood prepared for war before their lord ;
But the high Jove upbounded from his throne,
And roared forth, " Friends, but let the fool
    alone.
Lay down your weapons, patience, and be still ;
If so it please him he shall work his will."
As one the gods retired before their chief,
His words obeying though without belief.

Proudly that mortal went and took the sods,
Rejoiced that he had triumphed over gods,
He touched the shapeless heap with wondrous
 skill,
And taught the senseless clay to form his will.
Oh, miracle ! the workman's dauntless knife
Has given that mass the glorious form of life ;
Half frantic round that lovely form he ran,
Crying, " Behold, ye gods, I've formed a man."
He held the beauteous thing and kissed its cheek,
And prayed it almost tearfully to speak.
But, no ; it stayed unmoved, as cold as stone,
There was no soul,—the body there alone.
There was no man, no life, no mind, no breath ;
If like to man, then only like in death.

In latter days when Jove's career was o'er,
When heathen gods usurped the earth no more,
When deadly hates and feuds were well-nigh
 past,

S

Another man arose like to the last,
In high ambition and a soul for fame ;
But with a far more glorious heaven-born aim.
He strove not, vaunted not with his frail power,
To form a man the creature of an hour ;
For what is man, the noblest man, but earth,
Stung by vexations from the hour of birth ?
He longed to make a soul, yet it was not
A wild desire from pride or sin begot ;
But still he felt a longing past control,
To shadow faintly forth a human soul.
He raised a building vast and undefined,
To form an outer temple for the mind,
But all was bare within that giant place,
Nothing all round but dreary empty space ;
At length he called to help him in his toils,
The wise inhabitants of far-off soils.
He prayed of each, the virtues each possest,
The arts and sciences they loved the best.
Then England brought the God Machinery,

With stern Resolve and patient Industry.

From gladsome France Invention glittering went,

With Fancy's fair-haired children hither sent ;

And from Italia's struggling bloodstained land,

Came Sculpture leading Painting by the hand.

So each brought something from his treasured
store,

Of saintly virtues or of kingly lore,

Till all had tribute paid to that great mind ;

All, all but one, but one was left behind.

Yonder the one whom all the world disdains,

Yonder pale Greece stands, weeping in her
chains ;

Those chains of centuries she cannot break,

Weighed down her weary head as thus she
spake,

" And I have nought to give, no precious art,

No virtues springing from the inmost heart ;

Her people sunk in vice, her crown in shame,

Greece lives no longer—only lives in name."

Her voice went forth in one long piteous cry,
" I give my all, I give you memory."

And thus that soul was formed, yet not by one,
But by a thousand was the labour done.
But it *was* made, so fair, so pure, so bright,
Its spotless courts flung open to the sight.

Then the great man who formed it looked and
    saw
That all was fair, yet wanted something more ;
So sent his spirit soaring far above,
And spread o'er all the fair twins, Peace and
    Love.

THE STAR OF HOPE.

FAR around the night has gathered,
   Holding all in close embrace,
And the lovers in the garden
   Cannot see each other's face.

There beneath the porch are sitting
   Wife and husband side by side ;
As they talk the tears are stealing,
   Tears the darkness serves to hide.

Wandering lonely on the uplands,
  Stray I with a wavering tread,
With my eyes intently gazing
  On the blackness overhead.

Searching for one spot of brightness,
  Searching vainly near and far,
There amidst a cloud of thunder,
  Shines a little silver star.

And I gaze impassioned upward,
  On that star serene and kind;
And I think it looks with pity
  On my tempest shaken mind.

As I look the darkness brightens,
  And I feel my spirit glad;
Scarce I know as on I wander,
  Why before I was so sad.

Now I see a brilliant ball-room,
  With the dancers crowding near ;
There, amid that youth and beauty,
  Sits the one I hold so dear.

By her side there stands another,
  Him I hold in hate and dread ;
Now she laughs and smiles upon him,
  And I wish that I were dead.

Shining in at yonder casement,
  Gentle star so sweetly calm,
Be my shield, my guardian angel,
  Keep, oh ! keep me safe from harm.

Amy sees me ; yes, she calls me,
  And my foe has moved away,
While the star is shining brighter,
  Almost turning night to day.

Tossing on a bed of sickness,
    There I lie in maddening pain,
While my lips are wildly burning,
    And the fever racks my brain.

Smiling sadly down upon me,
    There my guardian star of yore,
And I feel my life returning,
    And my head is cool once more.

Who is she who kneels beside me,
    With her face upturned in pain?
" Amy, Amy, weep no longer,
    I return to earth again."

Sweet, oh! sweet, the kisses given
    In the face of newborn day;
Sweeter still the whispered promise,
    Amy, you are mine to-day.

Star of hope my guardian angel,
   In the midst of death and strife,
Guide me now, be with me ever,
   In the pilgrimage of life.

THE OLD HOME.

MANY memories pass me by,
Stop the pen and dim the eye;
Yesterday I went to see
What was once so dear to me,
Saw the home so long forgot,
Happy home where care was not.

Many, many years ago,
Years between of pain and woe,
Half in joy and half in grieving,
From that home I took my leaving;
And I saw it yesterday,—
Meadows where I used to play,

There the garden where I sowed,
Dug and laughed and raked and hoed,
With the ever sparkling rill,
And the roses blooming still,—
But in vain to pluck I tried
One, my little garden's pride ;
Stung the thorn my hand ungloved,
But the rose remained unmoved.

" Ah ! 'tis vain to grieve," I cried.
" That which once has been denied,
May return unthought-of pain,
Gladness never comes again.
Those who search for pleasures gone,
Snatch the rose and find the thorn."

THE DEATH OF THE SPY.

Wave the banners bright and high,
Fire the cannons to the sky,
Come with torch and dance and cry,
For to-day the spy must die.
      Spy, spy,
        He shall die.

Let our chorus meet his ear,
He shall quake and pale with fear,
For his doom that draweth near,
'Tis a doom both dark and drear.
      Spy, spy,
        He shall die.

He is caught, is caught at last,
Hold him, bind him, keep him fast,
All Dame Fortune's gifts are past,
And his star is overcast.
        Spy, spy,
        He shall die.

Though his schemes were deeply laid,
All his chances duly weighed,
Still he is our prisoner made,
And our labour far repaid.
        Spy, spy,
        He shall die.

He shall lie where cross roads meet,
With his head beside his feet ;
There to bide mid dust and heat,
Rotting in the wind and sleet.
        Spy, spy,
        He shall die.

A THOUGHT.

TELL me a thought, sweet May,
  That when I've wandered far,
To me it may come back,
  Like some mild shining star,
Upon my lonely track,
  To cheer me on my way.

At twilight's solemn hour
  That thought shall visit each,
Though oceans roll between
  And time o'erspreads the breach ;
The thought which once has been,
  Shall never lose its power.

Tell me a thought, my own,
  That thought which both shall bear;
Shall it be of the red, red rose,
  I planted in your hair,
That kissed your temple's snows,
  And nestled there alone?

Shall it be of the fiery sun,
  That sank beneath the sea?
The heavens were flaming red;
  We watched it from the lea,
Till all the light had fled,
  And darkness gathered on.

Shall it be of the silver old,
  We broke beside the mound;
The slender ribbon blue,
  We tied our necks around?
It held that symbol true,
  More precious far than gold.

To each the thought the same,
It matters little what,
Only at twilight hour,
To know I'm not forgot,
Since coin and sun and flower,
Are breathing forth my name.

REST.

THE weary tears are falling fast,
Tears shed for joys more prized since past,
But he lies there at rest at last.

He was so tired of earth's rude praise,
So weary of its lengthened ways,
But now he lies at rest always.

Weep not for him who lies so still,
For he is dead to nought but ill,
While sorrow holds you at her will.

T

You cannot tell the rest he feels,
Rest that all sin and sorrow seals,
All tears dries up, all sickness heals.

Oh! what a holy thing is rest,
Such the dove feels whose snow-white breast,
Presses once more the downy nest.

Forgetful of her journeys made,
The little ones beneath her laid,
She rests amid the tall wood's shade.

But few of human race there be,
Can feel on earth sweet rest like thee,
Thou thrice blest soul from pain set free.

Men whisper as that mound is past,
Where waving trees their shades have cast,
"Lie there, poor soul, at rest at last."

SONG.

THE rill went trickling to the brook,
  The brook went dashing to the sea,
A letter from my love it took,
  A letter from my love to me.

I dwell the glorious sea beside,
  Upon a wild unsought-for shore;
Before me lies the ocean wide,
  Its waves come rippling to my door.

My love he dwells on yonder hill,
  Full twenty furlongs from the sea;
He gave the letter to the rill,
  And so the letter came to me.

The white waves hastening to the beach,
 Came trickling, trickling to the land,
They laid a letter in my reach,
 And left it gently on the sand.

And when the rill had reached the brook,
 It bore a burden on its wave;
The murmuring brook that burden took,
 And to the sea that burden gave.

A little boat came sailing by,
 My love was standing on the deck,
The waves upbore him far and high,
 And left him clasped around my neck.

THE POET'S DESIRE.

In the summer light reposing,
  Lie I 'neath the larchen tree,
With the evening shadows closing,
  Dreaming what I wish to be.

High above the stars are gazing,
  Battling with the clouds for space,
Far apart in distance mazing,
  Shines forth each familiar face.

As the pale stars' lonely measure,
　So the streams of memory run;
From the haze of time and pleasure,
　Stealing forward one by one.

Not an anxious hurrying river,
　Nought shall bound and nought shall stop;
But a streamlet gliding ever,
　Trickling onward drop by drop.

Oft I've longed in verse to battle,
　With a poet's words of fire,
Driving down the meaner cattle,
　By the force of my desire.

Struggling on for greater glory,
　With my wearied restless soul,
Till an old man bowed and hoary,
　I should reach the wished-for goal.

But have done with idle prating,
 Life is far too short for all,
And the weary days of waiting
 Close around me like a pall.

Let me brave my lifetime lonely,
 Though I conquer, though I fall,
On my grave be written only,
 " Here lies one who gave his all."

ROBERT'S GRAVE.

" THE grass is wet with the tears that fall,
   Those tears that shall fall for aye,
And I lie beneath the churchyard wall,
   And shuddering shun the sky.

" Many have come to bid me go,
   To their words I have answered not,
For I know I am nearer to Robert so,
   And I will not leave the spot.

" He shall not be left to lie alone,
   In the churchyard cold and drear,
Though surely his heart was worse than stone,
   When he died and left me here.

" I will creep to his side where none shall see,
    And cover him with my gown ;
His grave-stone shall my pillow be,
    And the grass, my couch of down.

" I cannot reach to his pale, pale form,
    Nor fondle the locks I love,
But perhaps he may lie more safe and warm,
    If my body be stretched above.

" Would I might see his gentle face,
    For I know that he is not dead,
But the earth has covered his resting-place,
    And burdened his hallowed head.

" Deep blue eyes and an open brow,
    A forehead both broad and high,
I see him standing before me now,
    In the light of the evening sky.

" Some call me foolish and others mad,
    But I know it is not true ;
If sorrow and loss like mine they had,
    They would weep the whole year through.

" How fast the twilight is closing round,
    The shadows are sinking deep,
And I fear, O my love ! in the cold dark ground
    Thou hast fallen fast asleep."

Slowly she rose from the frozen mound,
    She has kissed it once and twice ;
She has taken her cloak and wrapt it round,
    For the night is cold as ice.

" Lie there, my Robert, so warm and still,
    And may thy sleep be cheery,
And when at morn thou hast slept thy fill,
    Thou wilt wake and find me near thee."

THE ILLUMINATION OF ST. PETER'S.

ALL in the silent night we left the door,
  And drove away through long deserted streets ;
The citizens must all be on before,
  For scarce a single muffled man one meets.

Across the ancient Tiber, rolling deep,
  Beside St. Angelo all rising bare,
And forth from out the ghostly night we leap
    Forth in the blaze of that world-wondrous
      square.

The few stray stars above rise faint and pale,
   Scared from their brightness by that scene
     more bright ;
Like Palace charmed in some old fairy tale,
   St. Peter's stands in one soft, silver light.

A little while, and then again a change ;
   That silvery light has turned to fiery gold ;
The softer shades amidst the crimson range,
   As silver glows red golden in the mould.

When first we saw it rising in the night,
   Soberly its light fell as the cold, calm moon ;
But now it towers erect as fair and bright
   As shines the Sun in those long days of June.

Yet scarce I find it in my heart to praise,
   Albeit it is so fair, so wondrous fair,
For somewhat in the scene has struck my gaze,
   And shown a dreary something wanted there.

The *City* lies in darkness sunk profound ;
　Above, the sky of coming thunder warns ;
Only St. Peter's sheds bright day around ;
　The Church rejoices but the City mourns.

I watch fair Rome so quiet beneath the skies,
　Shrinking in darkness from that brilliant light ;
I feel prophetic flame within me rise,
　I read her Future and her Past aright.

When first the Church sent forth her Lamp on
　　　earth,
　Humble she was, and held in low esteem,
Her anger mocked, her praise of little worth,
　Her glory laughed at as an idle dream.

Like the sweet shining of the silvery light,
　Before yon glorious golden glare arose,
With gentle lustre through the heathen night,
　She walked in holy peace and calm repose.

But Time went by, and with each circling year
　　Increased her splendour and her power to quell;
The proudest monarchs bowed their heads in fear,
　　And 'neath her wrath the mightiest conquerors
　　　fell.

Whole nations, like the moth around a flame,
　　Fluttered before her light, poor foolish things!
Lured by the dazzling glare, the blaze of fame,
　　They turned, they hovered close, and burnt
　　　their wings.

No more her lamp shone like the tranquil stream
　　Whereon the moon her pale reflection throws,
But like the summer sun's most angry beam
　　Fiercely she stood and scorched to death her
　　　foes.

Proud Church! your day is done, your glory past,
　　No longer shall you lord it o'er the globe;
Lay down your power, resign your rights at last,
　　And clothe your grandeur in her funeral robe.

In truth St. Peter's blaze is wondrous now,
  Its brilliancy illuminates the sky.
But see! the Day has reached Soracte's brow
  And ere an hour its radiancy must die.

When all is dark and night retains her sway,
  Even the glowworm is a light we prize ;
But we should spurn it from our feet away,
  Dared it to rival with the morning skies.

I see, I see adown the march of years
  The holy sun of Liberty arise !
St. Peter's lamp, drowned by a nation's tears,
  Quivers and falls and fades from mortal eyes.

Come, Hope of Italy, to your Mother Rome,
  In whose fond sheltering arms you grew to
      strength ;
Return, sweet Freedom, to your ancient home ;
  Take pity on a people's prayers at length !

Above the grave of servitude laid low,
 Italia's griefs shall shrink like ghosts away,
And all a nation rise unharmed by foe,
 To hail the first glad beam of Freedom's day!

Rome.

TRANSLATIONS FROM THE GERMAN.

U

FLOWERS. (*From Schiller.*)

O HAPPY blossoms of the field !
  O children of the April sun !
Whom loving Nature taught to yield,
  Such joy and sweetness every one.
Your dress is brave with woven light,
And gay the colours flashing bright,
  Which Flora stole from gods on high.
Yet weep, fair children of the spring ;
Sweethearts ! ye lack the noblest thing,—
  Soul-less ye live, and soul-less die.

The nightingales and larks may sing,
 Of love's sweet lot the live-long day,
Within your cups the elves may swing,
 And bill and coo their own wee way ;
And water-sprites below the lake,
Your laps for lovers' heads may take,
 Your fragrant crowns for lovers' sleep,
And love may come and love may go,
But love's sweet lot ye ne'er may know ;
 Then weep, ye pretty children, weep !

But when I pluck your blossoms bright,
 My love's ambassadors to me,
Though exiled I from Nanny's sight,
 Yet you, dear friends, shall speak for me.
And soul and heart, and life and speech,
My lover's touch shall give you each,
 Dumb messengers of fond despair !
And He the first of gods to men,
Within your leaves shall clamber then,
 And make his godhead's dwelling there.

EVENING'S DEVOTION   (*From Spitta.*)

How solemn is the evening tide!
How smilingly the day has died!
Now sing so reverently and long,
The forest birds their evening song.

The flowers indeed must silent rest,
Since with no voice the flowers are blest;
But all their fragrant heads are bowed
In wordless worship to the ground.

Where'er I go, where'er I look,
Rise prayers of evening ; in the brook
Lies, even there reflected thrown,
A whole blue heaven of its own.

All things that live and live aright,
Are praying for a holy night ;
And all are whispering softly now,
" O Child of Man, pray also thou ! "

THE HERALDS OF SPRING.

(From Hoffman von Fullersleben.)

To the merry larks the earth she said,
   That spring was come at last,
Then fluttering up to Heaven they sped,
   And sang of it loud and fast;
The green fields heard it and the wood,
   The meadow flowers and the streams,
Till the whole world had understood,
   And man amidst his dreams.
But man heard *last* what the larks had said,
And he only saw how the Spring lay dead.

LIGHT AND WARMTH. (*From Schiller.*)

THE noblest man with quiet trust,
  Steps through the world at morn,
He thinks the good within him must,
  By other hearts be borne ;
And consecrates with throbbing breast,
His faithful arm to Truth's behest.

Ah ! soon he finds the world how strong,
  How narrow and how vain,
Then seeks he only midst the throng,
  To shield himself from stain.
His heart in stony place shut fast,
Must close itself to love at last.

The beams of Truth aglow with light,
 Not always warmth impart ;
Thrice happy those whose opened sight,
 Has cost them not the heart ;
"Oh ! join to world-wide caution then,
A Christian's love for brother men.'

IN THE SPRING. (*From Sturm.*)

THE Spring she came on Zephyr's breath,
　　From mountain down to plain,
" Now though your sleep be deep as death,
　　Ye sleepers wake again."

Then stirred a thousand buds from sleep,
　　And strengthened hour by hour,
And swelled and pressed their prison deep,
　　And burst their nursling bower.

Then tender leaves of virgin green,
From nut-brown cradles sprung,
And timidly the boughs between
On slender stems they clung.

Then rose the snowdrop swift and wild,
From slumbers sweetly strong ;
She almost feared, that beauteous child,
She might have slept too long.

Then dormice came from underground,
Their lifeless rest was done ;
And gnats and beetles blazed around,
And sparkled in the sun.

Then raised her eyes the violet blue,
Which deep in grasses lies,
And primroses and cowslips too,
And white anemones.

And then my heart began to beat,
  So mournfully and fast,
And down my cheeks like harvest sleet,
  A stream of tears there past.

Of those I loved, I quietly thought,
  'Neath grassy hillocks lain,
Those whom the Spring with glory fraught,
  Can never wake again.

THE MAIDEN'S SONNET. *(From Schiller.)*

THE clouds are gathering,
   The oak glades roar,
  And the maiden sits
    On the ocean shore;
The waves are breaking with might, with might,
And she sighs a prayer in the darkening night,
   Her eyes with tears o'erflown.

  " My heart is withered,
   The world is bare,
  It holds no longer
    The bright and fair.
Summon, sweet Mary, thy child to thee,
Earth's crowning gift is passed for me,
   To live and to love I have known."

" In vain the torrent
    Of tears is shed,
For sorrow can never
    Awake the dead ;
Yet say what may comfort those who mourn,
When love's sweet days are for ever gone,
    And I grant it, the Empress of Heaven."

Let the useless torrent
    Of tears be shed,
Though sorrow can never
    Awake the dead ;
For the sweetest comfort to those who mourn,
When love's bright days are for ever gone,
    Is to weep for the love which is riven.

THE STRANGER MAIDEN. *(From Schiller.)*

DEEP in a vale poor swains among,
   Appeared with every bright Spring's change,
So soon as first the glad larks sung,
     maiden beautiful and strange.

She was not in the valley born,
   From whence she came they could not tell,
So soon were track and traces gone,
    When once the maiden said farewell.

And blest were all when she was by,
   She touched hearts with a golden key,
But yet a something proud and high.
    Repulsed familiarity.

She brought fresh fruits and summer flowers,
   Brought all from lands so far away ;
They bloomed in brighter climes than ours,
   In soils more beauteous and more gay.

And unto each her gifts she gave ;
   To some cool fruits, and flowers to some ;
The old man tottering to the grave,
   The youth, they all turned laden home.

Welcome with her was every guest ;
   But when there came a loving pair,
To them she gave her gifts the best,
   Her flowers most fragrant and most fair.

PRINTED BY TAYLOR AND CO.,
LITTLE QUEEN STREET, LINCOLN'S INN FIELDS.

Milton Keynes UK
Ingram Content Group UK Ltd.
UKHW012151270324
440282UK00003B/30